PELICAN BOOKS

A 229

WILLIAM JAMES

EDITED BY

MARGARET KNIGHT

William James

A SELECTION FROM HIS WRITINGS
ON PSYCHOLOGY

EDITED
WITH A COMMENTARY BY
Margaret Knight

PENGUIN BOOKS

Penguin Books Ltd, Harmondsworth, Middlesex

U.S.A. : Penguin Books Inc., 3300 Clipper Mill Road, Baltimore 11, Md
[*Educational Representative:*
D. C. Heath & Co., 285 Columbus Avenue, Boston 16, Mass]

AUSTRALIA : Penguin Books Pty Ltd, 762 Whitehorse Road,
Mitcham, Victoria

CANADA : Penguin Books (Canada) Ltd, 47 Green Street,
Saint Lambert, Montreal, P.Q.

SOUTH AFRICA : Penguin Books (S.A.) Pty Ltd, 218 Grand Parade Centre,
Adderley Street, Capetown

—

First published 1950
Reprinted 1954

MADE AND PRINTED IN GREAT BRITAIN
BY THE WHITEFRIARS PRESS LTD
LONDON AND TONBRIDGE

Contents

References and Abbreviations

Editorial Foreword

To write a 'Preface' to this book would be to act as a sort of chairman to a chairman, but someone must explain the distinctive office of the real chairman of the occasion. Margaret Knight here introduces William James in the first of a new series of Psychological Pelicans. The idea of this series is to present the great psychologists in accordance with the principle: *Let the man speak for himself*.

The intelligent reading public is getting tired, or ought to be getting tired, of having the ideas of Freud, Jung, Adler and of other psychologists reported only at second or third hand, and would like to know what these men actually said themselves. So it is proposed to present the major contributions to modern psychology through selected passages from the original texts. But the series will not be merely another collection of anthologies. Each will read as a continuous text – an ordered sequence of extracts, linked by a running commentary.

It was a happy chance that enabled this series to be opened by an account of the ideas of William James. James is the bridge in Psychology between the nineteenth and the twentieth centuries. He stands at the point of transition from a Psychology which was in fact a branch of Philosophy with some scientific trimmings to a genuinely scientific psychology with some philosophical entanglements. There is no comparable author whose roots run farther back and spread more widely, or whose branches stretch out further into the present. In the works of William James, the reader will feel the almost contemporary presence of the philosophical precursors of scientific psychology – of men like Locke, Berkeley and Hume. He will feel, too, the forcible impact upon this philosophical tradition of the great biologists, of Darwin and Huxley and of men like Herbert Spencer and Galton.

Looking in the other direction – into the present century – there will be found no textbook of the period of the *Principles of Psychology* which is less out of date at the present time; none more frequently quoted in contemporary texts, none of its day more frequently prescribed to contemporary students, none more resistant to the trends of scientific fashion. It is a book, too, which comes nearer than any other to achieving something like a synthesis of the characteristic features of the British, Continental and American ingredients in the mixture that is labelled 'Psychology'. It is characteristically British in its philosophical background, in tackling large theoretical issues from a common-sense empirical approach. It draws more freely upon Continental sources than did any British, or any other, text of its time. If it drew less freely from America itself, that is because in the eighteen nineties there was so little to draw upon. Rather, American psychology has had to draw on James. There is hardly a movement or interest of Psychology in the United States in which it is not possible to trace his influence. It was James who placed Psychology four-square upon a physiological foundation, and who systematically thought of behaviour in terms of response to stimulation. More significant of the genius of his nation for psychological studies than any of his special doctrines was the generally extraverted character of his scientific approach. Although the most brilliant and subtle practitioner of the art of introspection, he was, as befits a psychologist, more interested in others than he was in himself, and he was responsive to everything that lives. James Ward, his opposite number in Great Britain, had written, taking a phrase from Bishop Berkeley, that 'the whole choir of Heaven and furniture of earth' form part of the subject-matter of Psychology. But Ward did not mean by this what the plain man would naturally have taken him to mean. He, in common with most psychologists in Great Britain (always excepting Francis Galton) had a rather constricted view of what psychology is about. It was in America that the field of psychology became in practice co-extensive with human interest in behaviour as reflecting mind. This was the field of interest for James. True, James had his blind spots. In his textbook, he gives a sympathetic interpretation of the love of the she-bear for her mate and of the love of a hen for her egg, but apart from that there is not an awful lot concerning sex. But this was a blind spot common to all the textbooks prior to the age of Freud.

On the other hand, there was no textbook of his time containing a greater body of curious information about the unconscious mind. It was a common jibe that the older textbooks of Psychology really tell us very little that we did not know before. But some of the things that James had to tell the student of psychology might well have made the student's hair stand on end, not in terror (because for James human nature was something of a joke) but certainly in surprise. The *Principles of Psychology* appeared in 1890. To find a volume of comparable human interest one needs to go back to Galton's *Inquiries into Human Faculty* (1883) or forward to Freud's *Psychopathology of Everyday Life* (1904).

James is read, and will continue to be read, not only for the exciting content of his books, but also for his engaging style. The often quoted statement that, while his brother Henry wrote novels like psychology, he wrote psychology like novels betrays perhaps misunderstanding both of the writing of psychology and the writing of novels. Henry wrote novels in the way he thought they should be written, and many have since come to think that he was right. But that is precisely how William wrote psychology, and on that there is no one who disagrees with him. He wrote as though he supposed that human nature was a matter of interest to human beings, not merely as a 'proper' but as an irresistible study for mankind.

C. A. MACE

INTRODUCTION

Introduction

WILLIAM JAMES was born in New York on 11 January 1842. He was the eldest of five children, the others being Henry (the novelist) b. 1843; Garth Wilkinson ('Wilkie') b. 1845; Robertson ('Bob') b. 1846; and Alice, b. 1848. Their father, Henry James the elder, was a remarkable man – a 'character' in the full-blooded nineteenth century sense; and since he exerted an immense influence on his children's development, any account of William James must begin with his father.

Henry James senior was the son of an immigrant from Ulster, and was brought up in a Calvinist, Presbyterian atmosphere. At the age of twenty-four he entered Princeton Theological Seminary with the idea of becoming a Methodist minister, but he withdrew three years later, permanently alienated from the church. He never followed any profession. Many doors were, in any case, closed to him, since he was very lame, having lost a leg in boyhood in a courageous attempt to stamp out a fire; so, having a considerable independent income, he proceeded without qualms of conscience to live on it, and for the next few years led the life of a gentleman of leisure, reading, travelling, and visiting and corresponding with friends, who included Emerson, Wendell Holmes, and other well-known men of the day. He married at the age of twenty-nine, and William, the first child, was born two years later.

When Henry James senior was thirty-five, an event occurred which changed the course of his life. His friend Garth Wilkinson introduced him to the writings of Swedenborg, and these affected him with the force of a revelation. 'I read from the first' he said 'with palpitating interest ... [and I felt myself] lifted by a sudden miracle into felt harmony with universal man, and filled to the brim with the sentiment of indestructible life.' From that time on, his mission in life was decided; he devoted himself wholeheartedly to the study of Swedenborg, and to the spread of his doctrines by lecturing, writing, and otherwise proselytizing.

This account calls up a picture of a familiar type of crank, but the picture is far from complete. A crank Henry James certainly was, but he was a crank in the best sense of the word; that is to say, he had the tolerance, and the enthusiasm for ideas, that go with high intelligence, though he lacked the critical faculty that is the fruit of intellectual training. As a philosopher he was one of those who, to quote Perry, 'argued freely from analogy, took figures of speech literally, and produced a blend of poetry and science which was neither the one or the other.' [1] It might be urged in extenuation, however, that this is only what the amateur metaphysician always does; and that the same tendencies, employed in defence of orthodoxy, have made the reputation of many religious apologists.

There was one respect, fortunately, in which James was not a typical crank: he was not solemn. He had a keen and irreverent sense of humour, and his literary style at its best was vigorous, witty and trenchant—in fact, not unlike that of William James himself. His most attractive productions are not his Swedenborgian writings,[2] but his letters, of which a number are quoted by Perry. The following impression of a visit to England gives a taste of his style. 'On the whole [we] have seen much that is

---

1. Perry, I, 150–1.
2. As W. D. Howells remarked 'Henry James wrote *The Secret of Swedenborg*, and kept it'.

admirable and lovable in brother Bull, and especially in sister Cow. There is no nobler ingredient going into the new humanity than that which comes out of these shy, sullen, honest men, and these ill-drest, energetic, long-striding and unaffected women.' [3]

From our present point of view the most important characteristic of Henry James senior is that he was an almost perfect father. He had five children, all highly intelligent, high-spirited and argumentative; and he appears to have achieved the remarkable feat of bringing them up without ever telling them that father knew best. He was a firm believer in children's thinking for them-selves, and forming their views in the give-and-take of intellectual combat; and his sons grew up quite unham-pered by the notion that it is rude to contradict. A family friend, Edward Emerson, gives an amusing picture of meal-times in the James household:

'The adipose and affectionate Wilkie', as his father called him, would say something and be instantly corrected or disputed by the little cock-sparrow, Bob, the youngest, but good-naturedly defend his statement, and then Henry (Junior) would emerge from his silence in defence of Wilkie. Then Bob would be more impertinently insistent, and Mr James would advance as moderator, and William, the eldest, join in. The voice of the moderator presently would be drowned by the combatants and he soon came down vigorously into the arena, and when, in the excited argument, the dinner knives might not be absent from eagerly gesticulating hands, dear Mrs James, more conventional, but bright as well as motherly, would look at me, laughingly reassuring, saying, 'Don't be disturbed, Edward; they won't stab each other. This is usual when the boys come home.' [4]

3. Perry, I, 120.
4. Perry, I, 171–2.

Perry adds:

I have been informed by another and surviving witness of these family scenes that there was a certain method in this seeming madness. The father would propound some provocative idea, and throw it into the midst of his brood in order that they might sharpen their teeth on it and, in their eagerness to refute him or one another, exercise themselves in the art of combative thinking.[4]

The effect of the family atmosphere on the James children would be difficult to exaggerate. What gave this atmosphere its unique quality was the combination of unsparing and high-spirited criticism with intense family affection. The Jameses were an unusually devoted family, and they expressed their feelings for one another with an unselfconscious demonstrativeness that suggests their Irish ancestry. Here, for example, is how Henry James senior concluded a letter to his two eldest sons, then aged 30 and 31: 'Good-bye, my lovely boys. I have been hearing so many things about you both of late, apropos of Willy's going away, that I am quite set up. Your loving Daddy.'[5] It was in this atmosphere of affectionate security that the intellectual skirmishes of the James family were conducted; and the result was, that though to an outsider they might seem to be hitting hard, they never hit to hurt.

The following are two vintage specimens of the Jamesian brand of good-humoured intellectual ragging. When Henry James senior was about to publish a work entitled *Substance and Shadow: or Morality and Religion in their Relation to Life*, William designed a decorative woodcut for the title-page; this represented a man flogging a dead horse. Wilkie, the third son, writing home to his family during the American Civil War, when he was an

4. Perry, I, 171–2.
5. Among the last words spoken by Henry James on his deathbed were: 'Oh, I have such good boys — *such* good boys.'

officer in a Negro regiment, ended as follows: 'Tell Harry (i.e. Henry James the novelist) that I am waiting anxiously for his "next". I can find a large sale for any blood-and-thunder tale among the darks.'

Brought up as they were, it probably never occurred to the James children that there were people who regarded intellectual discussion as dull or priggish. To them it was fun, it was exciting, it was one of the most amusing ways in which one could possibly spend one's time: and this attitude pervades William James's writings, which have a quality of high spirits and intellectual exhilaration that makes them supremely readable even when they are dealing with the most difficult and abstract subjects. This tendency disturbed certain critics, who felt that, though the *Principles of Psychology* was undoubtedly a work of genius, a standard textbook ought by rights to be somewhat duller. Sully, for example, reviewing the *Principles* in *Mind*, remarked in a mildly scandalized tone that though there was nothing unseemly in 'the introduction into psychology of a little imagination, or for that matter, a spice of humour' yet there might be so much of 'dazzling effect' as to blur 'the sharp boundaries of scientific thought'. Again, 'For [James's] rollicking defiance of the authorities . . . the reader of many dull psychologies may well be thankful, and yet he may wish here and there for just a *soupçon* of the old spirit which has prompted mankind at all stages of culture to pay reverence to ancestors'.[6] Henry James's comment on this and similar criticisms was, 'they don't understand intellectual larking'.

Another important formative influence on the James children was travel. As Perry says, 'Travel was a fundamental fact in the history of the James family. It was habitually resorted to as a means of education for the

young, and as a remedy for the old, whatever their affliction, whether of body or mind'.[7] William James made his
first trip to Europe at the age of two-and-a-half, and from
then until his death at sixty-seven he only once spent as
long a period as six years continuously in America. The
young Jameses' nomadic childhood meant that their education was, to put it mildly, irregular. Until he was nine,
William was entrusted to a series of governesses; from nine
to thirteen he attended three different schools in New
York. His father, however, had been growing increasingly
dissatisfied with American schools, and in 1855 he decided
to take all the children to Europe, thus 'allowing them to
absorb French and German and get a better sensuous
education than they are likely to get here'. A few months
later they embarked; and one may spare a passing thought
of sympathy for the unfortunate Mrs James, setting out
on travels of indefinite duration, with a lame husband and
five children under fourteen. After a brief visit to London
they settled in Switzerland, where William, Henry and
Wilkie were established at a 'polyglot pensionnat' in
Geneva. But this establishment proved disappointing on
closer acquaintance, and two months later they were all
back in London, accompanied by the first of a series of
French governesses. In the next five years, William
attended educational establishments in Paris, Boulogne,
Rhode Island, Geneva and Bonn.

It was an unusual educational programme, but it proved
more successful than might have been expected. William
emerged from it, it is true, with a rooted dislike of mathe-
matics and logic, and a conviction (which was almost
certainly unjustified) of his incapacity for both subjects.
But he had read widely and critically; he could speak
French fluently and German reasonably well; his intellec-

7. Perry, I, 177.

tual curiosity was unblunted; and, what is not less important, he had already acquired the cosmopolitan culture and
breadth of outlook that distinguished him throughout his
life. James was, in the best sense of the word, a man of the
world. Though he frequently and proudly proclaimed
himself a 'Yankee', he had absorbed the traditions of
Europe; and though he was an intellectual *par excellence*,
he was far from conforming to the stock picture of the
intellectual as socially difficult and practically inept. He
had plenty of *savoir-faire*; he knew his way about; and he
got on easily with all types of people – a gift that not all
psychologists have possessed.

The immediate result of these unconventional *Lehr-
jahren* was the announcement by William that he had had
enough of formal education and that he wished to become
a painter. Poor Mr James thought this a deplorable
decision, but, characteristically, it did not occur to him to
oppose it; and, the family being at that time in Europe,
they all returned to America so that William could study
under the artist of his choice, William Morris Hunt. But
the policy of non-interference proved in this case to have
been a wise one. In less than a year, William decided that
he had mistaken his vocation ('there is nothing on earth
more deplorable than a bad artist'), and the autumn of 1861
found him, at the age of nineteen, enrolled as a student of
chemistry at the Lawrence Scientific School at Harvard.

There, for some time, he pursued the study of chemistry
with considerable interest and success, despite the fact that
his instructor described him as 'not wholly devoted to the
study of chemistry' and as 'irregular in his attendance at
laboratories'. After a year or so, however, his interest began
to shift in the direction of the biological sciences. This was
due largely to the influence of Professor Louis Agassiz,
who was one of the most striking personalities at Harvard,

and whose lectures on Natural History had impressed James deeply. In 1863, accordingly, he transferred from the Department of Chemistry to the Department of Comparative Anatomy and Physiology.

But he was now twenty-one, and the problem of the choice of a career was becoming urgent. He discussed the possibilities in various letters to his family: the following, to his cousin Kitty, was written in September 1863: 'I am obliged before the 15 January to make finally and irrevocably "the choice of a profession". I suppose your sex . . . has no idea of the awful responsibility of such a choice. I have four alternatives: Natural History, Medicine, Printing, Beggary. Much may be said in favour of each. I have named them in the ascending order of their pecuniary invitingness. After all, the great problem of life seems to be how to keep body and soul together, and I *have* to consider lucre. To study natural science, I know I should like, but the prospect of supporting a family on $600 a year is not one of those rosy dreams of the future with which the young are said to be haunted. Medicine would pay, and I should still be dealing with subjects which interest me – but how much drudgery and of what an unpleasant kind is there! Of all departments of Medicine, that to which Dr Prince devotes himself is, I should think, the most interesting.'[8] (Dr Prince, Kitty's husband, was a psychiatrist.) In another letter, written to his mother, he said that if he had only himself to consider he would not hesitate to choose science, 'but it seems hard on Mrs W. J., "that not impossible she", to ask her to share an empty purse and a cold hearth.'[9]

Eventually the choice was made for medicine, and he entered the Harvard Medical School in the autumn of 1864. But it was clear from the first that the choice was not a wholehearted one. Though James was deeply interested in physiology (particularly in the physiology of the nervous system), the idea of being a practising doctor was always distasteful to him. However, even his physiological studies were not destined to continue for long. The following year, Professor Agassiz was to lead a party of field naturalists on an expedition up the Amazon river. A number of students were going, and it was suggested that William should join the party.

In the James family, the decision was a foregone conclusion. It would mean postponing William's graduation for a year or so, but this was no great matter: and (who knows)? perhaps after all his vocation was to be a biologist or a naturalist rather than a doctor – in any case, the expedition would give him a chance to find out. So his medical studies were shelved temporarily, and he sailed with Agassiz in April 1865.

The expedition did indeed prove instructive, though not quite in the way expected. It soon became clear to William that he was not intended for a field naturalist. 'If there is one thing I hate' he wrote to his father 'it is collecting. I don't think it is suited to my genius at all. . . . I am convinced now for good that I am cut out for a speculative rather than an active life'.[10] Furthermore, he found his travelling companions very dull ('Except for Tom Ward I don't care if I never see one of 'em again'). They appear to have been earnest young men with a zeal for accumulating facts, but with no interest in cosmic speculation, and James felt starved for the sort of discussion he was used to at home. Then, to add to his troubles, he fell ill, with a complaint which was diagnosed at the time as smallpox,

10. These sentiments doubtless evoked a strong response in Henry James senior, who wrote of himself: 'The bent of my nature is towards affection and thought rather than action. . . . Moments spent in original deed, such as putting a button upon my coat . . . weigh very heavily upon my shoulders.'

but which appears to have been varioloid. Whatever it was, it left him weak and exhausted, and, for a time, made it impossible for him to read or to use his eyes. He became very depressed, and would gladly have returned home at once had it been possible. However, he was obliged to go on, and towards the end of the expedition, his health and spirits improved and he began to feel that the year had been far from wasted. Nevertheless, he was thankful to get home. 'I thrill with joy,' he wrote to his family 'when I think that one short month and we are homeward bound. Welcome my native slosh and ice and cast-iron stoves, magazines, theatres, friends and everything! even churches! . . . I long to be back to books, studies, etc., after this elementary existence. . . . Tell Harry that I long to see him, and hear him, and read him, as one seasick longs for land; and Father . . . I feel as if I could talk to him night and day for a week.'[11]

James resumed his medical studies in March 1866; but they were soon interrupted once more. The following autumn, shortly after starting on an 'internship' at the Massachusetts General Hospital, he began to suffer from a variety of health troubles. In the words of his son, 'Insomnia, digestive disorders, eye troubles, weakness of the back, and sometimes deep depression of spirits, followed one another or afflicted him simultaneously'.[12] No physical cause was found for any of these conditions, apart from the eye trouble, which was attributed to the after-effects of his illness on the Agassiz expedition.

A modern psychologist, confronted with such a string of miscellaneous functional disorders, would at once suspect that the cause was mainly emotional; and there can be little doubt that this was in fact the case. A certain

delicacy of nervous constitution seems to have been hereditary in the James family. Alice, the youngest, spent the
last years of her life in a state of invalidism which, even in
those days, was diagnosed as mainly neurotic; and, to a
lesser extent, her brothers showed the same tendency to
convert their mental conflicts into physical symptoms.
The nature of William's conflict is not hard to surmise.
He had never been happy about the choice of medicine as a
profession, and the change from theoretical studies to the
grim realities of hospital life in the 'sixties may well have
confirmed him in his feeling that he had made a disastrous
mistake. But he was now twenty-four; he had made two
false starts already; another change of plan would surely
reveal him as hopelessly unstable. It is in just such states
of indecision and conflict that psychogenic symptoms tend
to develop.

In 'psychosomatic' illness, as it is now commonly called,
unconscious imitation often plays a part in the selection of
symptoms, and this seems to have been the case with
William's backache. Henry was the first of the family to
suffer with his back, and he and William exchanged
frequent letters in which they described and compared
their symptoms. The trouble in Henry's case was attributed to a mysterious injury that he received when he was
eighteen. The exact nature of this injury is impossible to
determine, since Henry's account is, even for him,
obscure: indeed, the hushed and portentous tone in which
he refers to the incident has suggested to some readers that
it left him sexually impotent. Actually, however, all that
appears to have happened is that he strained his back
slightly when helping to put out a fire with a hand-pump.
But both the time and the circumstances of the event were
highly significant. The time was 1861 – just after the
outbreak of the American Civil War, when young men of

advanced views were flocking to join the Federal armies. The circumstances have already been stated; Henry was putting out a fire. It was in just such circumstances that Henry James senior sustained the injury that debarred him from active life.

Reading between the lines of the remarkable three pages of *Notes of a Son and a Brother* that Henry devotes to this incident,[13] few readers in these more psychologically sophisticated days can be in doubt of the facts: a trifling strain was magnified into a 'spinal injury' that made it impossible for Henry to serve in the army (William's 'delicacy' was by this time so well established that there seems to have been no question of military service in his case). Five years later, when it was William's turn to retreat into illness as an escape from an unpleasant future, it was not surprising that back trouble ('this family weakness') should be among the symptoms unconsciously selected.

Whatever might be the cause of William's troubles, no member of the James family could be in doubt of the appropriate treatment. If William was ill, then, obviously,

13. The following are among the more lucid of Henry's statements : 'Jammed into the acute angle between two high fences, where the rhythmic play of my arms in tune with that of several other pairs, but at a dire disadvantage of position, induced a rural, a rusty, a quasi-extemporized old engine to work and a saving stream to flow, I had done myself, in face of a shabby conflagration, a horrid even if an obscure hurt : and what was interesting from the first was my not doubting in the least its duration. . . . The interest of it I very presently knew would certainly be of the greatest, would even in conditions kept as simple as I might make them become little less than absorbing.' 'Scarce at all to be stated . . . the queer fusion or confusion established in my consciousness during the soft spring of '61 by the firing on Fort Sumter, Mr Lincoln's instant first call for volunteers and [the] physical mishap already referred to as having overtaken me at the same dark hour.' (pp. 296–9). These passages are perhaps unique among Henry's writings in that they reveal more than the author intended.

William must go to Europe. The suggestion suited William well, since it would enable him to take medicinal baths and other forms of spa treatment that were not available in America, while he continued to study along the lines of his main interest – the physiology of the nervous system – in which German universities were at that time leading the world. He set off accordingly in the spring of 1867, and spent the next two years in Europe, mainly in Germany.

On the whole they were two very miserable years. Life in solitary lodgings in a foreign town is not the ideal treatment for a young man suffering from depression, and there can be no doubt that, throughout most of his exile, William was homesick, bored and lonely in the extreme. One way in which he consoled his solitude was by letter-writing. The James family, fortunately for their biographers, were all voluminous correspondents, and William's output reached its high-water-mark during this period. He wrote long controversial screeds to his father, with whom he could still not resist arguing, though it had long been obvious that they could never see eye to eye; and to the family in general he wrote accounts of his doings and impressions which, despite his low spirits, were often brilliantly amusing. He had much to say, for example, about the German character, and the 'incredible capacity' of some German *savants* for 'seeing everything in the universe and out of it except the point'. In various letters he referred to his struggles with the German language, whose difficulties were 'quite unjustifiably great for a modern language – it is in fact without *any* of the modern improvements'. 'The profounder and more philosophical German [writer] requires that you shall bring all the resources of your nature, of every kind, to a focus, and hurl them again and again at the sentence, till at last you feel something give way, as it were, and the Idea begins to unravel itself.'[14]

However, as he explained in another letter, the language had its advantages for the writer, if not for the reader. 'The language allows and invites speculation and expatiation without limit. As soon as the first glimmering of an idea has dawned upon you, there is no reason why you should not begin to inscribe, for you can wallow round and round as you proceed, affixing limitations, lugging in definitions and explanations as fast as they suggest each other, and need never go back to re-shape your beginning. While with us you will, as a rule, come to grief if you begin your sentence without a pretty distinct idea of what the whole is going to be.'[15]

In the intervals of his studies, William seems to have spent a good deal of time in that perennial pursuit of lonely young men in 'digs' – looking out of the window at the girls in the houses opposite. As he wrote to the family;

Since my last I have discovered another lovely *vis-à-vis* [who] forms now . . . the consolation of my life. Every evening she sits in her window looking down upon me while I sit looking up at her, and from the modest blush that mantles on her cheek and the ill-repressed smile that gladdens her countenance, it is evident to me that she views me not with perfect indifference. I went down into the market this morning to purchase a bouquet to send to her, but the commissionaires, or *Dienstleute* as they call them here, were all such dirty ragamuffins to serve as Cupid's messengers, and I felt so bashful about buying the bouquet and asking one of them to take it to her, and moreover it was so doubtful whether, in the present state of our acquaintance, she would receive it, that I beat a humiliating retreat back to my room – where I now am. So you see, with all my solitude and reading, Aunt Kate could hardly say I dwell more in the Intellect than in the Affections.[16]

In writing to his family James adopted a deliberately light-hearted tone, to avoid causing anxiety, but in his letters to friends he was more outspoken. 'Sickness and solitude' he wrote to Tom Ward 'make a man into a mere lump of egotism without eyes or ears for anything external, and I . . . have rarely passed such an empty four months as the last.'[17] In another letter to Tom Ward, he said that in his first winter abroad he was continually on the verge of suicide. He even mentioned suicide in one letter to his father, though here he put it differently. 'Although I cannot exactly say that I got low-spirited, yet thoughts of the pistol, the dagger and the bowl began to usurp an unduly large part of my attention, and I began to think that some change . . . was necessary.'[18]

Two events of some importance occurred during these melancholy two years. William had his first literary effort published, and he showed the first clear signs of an interest in psychology. The literary effort was a review of a novel by H. Grimm. This William sent to Henry, together with a lurid account of the agonies endured in composing it, requesting his brother to read the review and 'if, after correcting the style and thoughts, with the aid of Mother, Alice and Father, and rewriting it if possible, you judge it to be capable of interesting in any degree anyone in the world but H. Grimm, himself, to send it to the *Nation* or the *Round Table*. I feel,' he added, 'that a living is hardly worth being gained at this price.'[19] How far Henry fulfilled these instructions is unknown, but the notice duly appeared in the *Nation*. William's psychological interests were first mentioned in a letter to Tom Ward. 'It seems to me that

16. Perry, I, 240.   17. Perry, I, 244.
18. LWJ, I, 96–7.   19. LWJ, I, 103.

perhaps the time has come for psychology to begin to be a science — some measurements have already been made in the region lying between the physical changes in the nerves and the appearance of consciousness (in the shape of sense perceptions), and more may come of it. I am going on to study what is already known, and perhaps may be able to do some work at it.'[20]

After two years, as his physical condition showed little improvement, James decided to return home. 'I believe', he wrote, 'I have a better chance of getting well in the quiet of home than in tossing about Europe like a drowned pup about a pond in a storm.' So he returned to America in November 1868 (he was now nearly twenty-seven), and once more took up his interrupted medical course.

However, his illness had served what was almost certainly its unconscious purpose — it was now taken for granted, by him and by everyone else, that though it would be a good thing to complete his medical degree, it would be quite out of the question for him ever to practise. It was considered impossible for him even to do laboratory work, since the state of his back precluded long hours of standing; and his idea seems to have been that he would 'pick up a precarious living by doing work for medical periodicals or something of that kind'. January 1869 found him hard at work preparing for his finals, which were due in six months. He wrote regretfully to a friend that he was obliged to restrict his reading mainly to medical subjects. 'Nevertheless, I do find time to read a little outside the required grooves.' A letter to Henry written some months later suggests that the last sentence was something of an understatement. 'I have been reading for recreation since you left a good many German books, Steffens' and C. P. Moritz's autobiographies, some lyric poetry, W. Humboldt's letters, Schmidt's *History of German Literature*, etc., which have brought to a head the slowly maturing feeling of the importance of German culture.'[21] This was written three weeks before his final examinations. Nevertheless, despite these distractions, he passed without difficulty ('midwifery gave me some embarrassment', he wrote, 'but the rest was trifling enough'), and in 1869 he became William James, M.D. This was the only academic degree that he ever gained by examination.

His troubles, however, were by no means over. He was not considered well enough to do any regular work, and for the next three years he remained at home, writing occasional odd articles and reviews, and most of the time in a state of hypochondriacal misery. It was not an entirely sterile period of his life, since he read voraciously, despite his supposed eye weakness; but, like many highly intelligent young men who have not enough to do, he become over-introspective and oppressed by philosophic doubt. It was at some time during these unhappy three years that he had the terrifying near-hallucinatory experience that he described in the chapter on 'The Sick Soul' in the *Varieties of Religious Experience*. (It is there disguised as the report of an anonymous 'French correspondent', but James later admitted that the experience was his own.)

Whilst in this state of philosophic pessimism and general depression of spirits about my prospects, I went one evening into a dressing-room in the twilight . . . when suddenly there fell upon me without any warning, just as if it came out of the darkness, a horrible fear of my own existence. Simultaneously there arose in my mind the image of an epileptic patient whom I had seen in the asylum, a black-haired youth with greenish skin, entirely idiotic, who used to sit all day on one of the benches, or rather shelves, against the wall, with his knees drawn up against his chin, and the coarse gray undershirt, which was his only garment, drawn over them, inclosing his entire figure. He sat there like a sort of sculptured Egyptian cat or Peruvian mummy, moving nothing but his black eyes and looking absolutely non-human. This image and my fear entered into a species of combination with each other. *That shape am I*, I felt, potentially. Nothing that I possess can defend me against that fate, if the hour for it should strike for me as it struck for him. There was such a horror of him, and such a perception of my own merely momentary discrepancy from him, that it was as if something hitherto solid within my breast gave way entirely, and I became a mass of quivering fear. After this the universe was changed for me altogether. I awoke morning after morning with a horrible dread at the pit of my stomach, and with a sense of the insecurity of life that I never knew before, and that I have never felt since. It was like a revelation; and although the immediate feelings passed away, the experience has made me sympathetic with the morbid feelings of others ever since. It gradually faded, but for months I was unable to go out into the dark alone.[22]

That James recovered from such a seriously morbid condition without psychiatric assistance is a testimony to the strength of his character – and to the power of ideas. Among the main factors contributing to his depression were the materialistic convictions induced by his medical training. Intellectually, he could see no escape from the 'automaton theory' – the view that our mental experiences are all physically produced, and that causal efficacy does not reside in conscious states as such, but in the brain states that produced them. Most people find this view disturbing when it is first put before them, and it was particularly so to James, since he mistakenly supposed it to imply that his depression could only be cured by physical treatment; if that failed (as it apparently had failed), nothing else could be done. From this impasse he was rescued by his reading of the French philosopher Renouvier. Renouvier converted him to a belief in mental causation; and from this time on, he ceased to regard his depression as something to be fatalistically endured, but took active steps to combat it by psychological means.[23]

His discovery of Renouvier marked the end of the worst period of James's depression, but it was two more years before he had sufficiently recovered to think of regular work. The President of Harvard University at that time was Charles W. Eliot, who ten years before had been James's instructor in chemistry at the Lawrence Scientific School. He was, in fact, that very instructor who had described James as irregular in his attendance at laboratories; but James had evidently made an impression, for when the post of Instructor in Physiology at Harvard fell vacant in 1872 Eliot offered it to James, and James accepted.

The decision marked a turning point in his life. Letters written at this time show the immense improvement in his health and spirits. Thus he wrote to Henry: 'The appointment to teach physiology is a perfect God-send to me just now, an external motive to work, which yet does not strain me — a dealing with men instead of my own mind, and a diversion from those introspective studies which had bred a sort of philosophical hypochondria in me of late and which it will certainly do me good to drop for a year.'[24] 'It is a noble thing for one's spirits to have some responsible work to do. I enjoy my revived physiological reading greatly.'[24] 'I find the work very interesting and stimulat-

---

23. The importance of Renouvier in James's development was more than therapeutic, for he may be said to have been the parent of that modified interactionism which became one of James's cardinal doctrines. (*Cf.* pp. 69–71.)

24. LWJ, I, 167.

ing. It presents two problems, the intellectual one -- how best to state your matter to [the students]; and the practical one -- how to govern them, stir them up, not bore them, yet make them work, etc. I should think it not unpleasant as a permanent thing. The authority is at first rather flattering to one. So far, I seem to have succeeded in interesting them, for they are admirably attentive, and I hear expressions of satisfaction on their part.'[25]

James had found his vocation at last. The next spring his appointment, which had originally been for one year only, was offered for renewal on a permanent basis, with the addition of a course in Anatomy. James hesitated for some time before accepting the offer, since he still felt the pull of philosophy; but he finally came to the conclusion, which he recorded in his diary, that 'Philosophical activity *as a business* is not normal for most men, and not for me. . . . To make the *form* of all possible thought the prevailing *matter* of one's thought breeds hypochondria. Of course my deepest interest will, as ever, lie with the most general problems. But . . . my strongest moral and intellectual craving is for some stable reality to lean upon. . . . That gets reality for us in which we place our responsibility, and the concrete facts in which a biologist's responsibilities lie form a fixed basis from which to aspire as much as he pleases to the mastery of universal questions when the gallant mood is on him.'[26] He accepted the permanent post and (after one more brief visit to Europe) continued for the next three years to teach anatomy and physiology with increasing success and self-confidence. In 1876 he offered a new course -- the first of its kind in America -- on physiological psychology; and, by securing the use of two small rooms in which to house psychological apparatus, he founded, almost without realizing it, the first laboratory for experimental psychology in the United States.

In another direction, too, 1876 was a momentous year, for it was in this year that James met, through a mutual friend, a Miss Alice Gibbens. The day after their meeting, he announced in a letter to Wilkie that he had seen 'the future Mrs W. J.'; and though it took nearly two years to convert Miss Gibbens to this view, James succeeded eventually, and they were married in July 1878, after a short engagement.

James's marriage was the second great turning-point of his life. Mrs James was a remarkable woman in her own right. She entered with understanding and sympathy into all James's interests, intellectual as well as personal, so that, in her absence, he described himself as 'deprived of the wonted ear into which to pour all my observations, aphorisms, wishes and complaints'. She introduced a necessary element of organization into his life, protected him from interruptions and distractions, and dissuaded him from squandering his nervous energy in too many directions at once. The effect on James was remarkable. The last traces of his hypochondria disappeared. Though he was always 'highly strung', and still suffered intermittently from eyestrain (probably the only one of his complaints that had any physical basis), the mysterious back weakness was seldom mentioned again: and from that time on, he accomplished an amount of work which, in the words of his son, 'would have astonished anyone who had known him only during the early 'seventies, and that would have honoured the capacity and endurance of any man'.

About a month before his marriage, James had entered into a contract with Henry Holt & Co. to produce a book on Psychology for a forthcoming American Science Series. In the preliminary correspondence, he remarked regret-

fully that he did not think he could undertake to complete
the book in less than two years. It actually took eleven
years, being published in 1890. However, James lost no
time in starting – he began to draft the opening chapters
on his honeymoon; and to a friend, Francis Child, who
appears to have made some humorous comments, James
wrote as follows: 'What is this mythological and poetical
talk about psychology and Psyche and keeping back a
manuscript composed during a honeymoon? The only
Psyche now recognized by science is a decapitated frog
whose writhings express deeper truths than your weak-
minded poets ever dreamed. *She* (not Psyche but the bride)
loves all these doctrines which are quite novel to her mind,
hitherto accustomed to all sorts of mysticisms and super-
stitions. She swears entirely by reflex action now, and
believes in universal *Nothwendigkeit.*'[27] (i.e. determinism).

The Jameses' first child, Henry James the third, was
born a year after their marriage. They had four children
(a fifth died in infancy), who all appear to have been
brought up in the authentic Jamesian tradition of argument
and travel. William, perhaps, did not take quite so enthusiastically to parenthood as his own father. Old Mr James
had the great advantage of having no profession, and so
could devote most of his time to his children; but William
had to try to fit them in among a thousand other preoccu-
pations, and he appears at times to have found it something
of a strain. 'I find', he wrote after the birth of his first
child, 'the cares of a nursing father to be very different
from those of a bachelor. Farewell the tranquil mind!'
But the sternest test came some years later. In 1892 James
had a year's leave of absence; and, having then four children aged from thirteen to two years, he blithely set off
with the whole family for Europe like his father before

him. From Switzerland his wails of disillusionment travelled home.

How could [you] see us go off and not raise a more solemn word of warning? It seems to me that the most solemn duty *I* can have in what remains to me of life will be to save my inexperienced fellow beings from ignorantly taking their little ones abroad when they go for their own refreshment. To combine novel anxieties of the most agonizing kind about your children's education, nocturnal and diurnal contact of the most intimate sort with their shrieks, their quarrels, their questions, their rollings-about and tears, in short, with all their emotional, intellectual and bodily functions, in what practically in these close quarters amounts to one room – to combine these things [I say] with a *holiday* for *oneself* is an idea worthy to emanate from a lunatic asylum. The wear and tear of a professorship for a year is not equal to one week of this sort of thing. . . . Alice, if she writes to you, will (after her feminine fashion) gloze over this aspect of our existence, because she has been more or less accustomed to it all these years and *on the whole does not dislike it* (!!), but I for once will speak frankly and not disguise my sufferings. Here in this precipitous Alpine village we occupy rooms in an empty house with a yellow-plastered front and an iron balcony above the street. . . . On that iron balcony all the innermost mysteries of the James family are blazoned and bruited to the entire village. *Things* are dried there, quarrels, screams and squeals rise incessantly to Heaven, dressing and undressing are performed, punishments take place – recriminations, arguments, execrations – with a publicity after which, if there *were* reporters, we should never be able to show our faces again. And when I think of that cool, spacious and quiet mansion lying untenanted in Irving Street, with a place in it for everything, and everything in its place when *we* are there, I could almost weep for 'the pity of it'.[28]

But this is to anticipate. In 1880, James underwent transmutation from Assistant Professor of Physiology to

28. LWJ, I, 321–2.

Assistant Professor of Philosophy. The change was little more than titular, as for some years he had lectured mainly on physiological psychology, and psychology at that time was still officially treated as a branch of philosophy. In 1885 he became Professor of Philosophy.

Among James's colleagues in the Philosophy Department were Josiah Royce, and (later) Hugo Münsterberg. The history of his relations with these two men is so characteristic as to be worth relating in detail. In 1877, the year before his marriage, James was visited at Harvard by an uncouth young philosophy student from Johns Hopkins University. This was Josiah Royce: who was then permitted, apparently for the first time in his life, to 'pour out his soul to somebody who really seemed to believe that a young man could rightfully devote his life to philosophy if he chose'. James divined the real intellectual distinction beneath the young man's superficial 'queerness', and gave him support and encouragement that Royce never forgot. In the following year, Royce was appointed to a lectureship in the University of California; but his fixed ambition was to work at Harvard with James and, four years later, in 1882, the opportunity presented itself. James (then Assistant Professor of Philosophy) was entitled to a sabbatical year, and someone was required to deputise in his absence. It was a temporary appointment, and carried only half-pay; but whoever took it had, in James's phrase, 'the inside track' for a permanent appointment that was soon to fall vacant. James wrote to Royce somewhat tentatively offering him the post, and Royce accepted enthusiastically. The absence of Palmer (then Professor of Philosophy) made it possible to renew his temporary appointment for a second year; and in the following year Palmer retired, James himself became Professor of Philosophy, and Royce stepped into his place as Assistant

Professor. Thus began what was probably the closest and most intimate friendship of James's life. More will be said of it later, but for the moment we must turn to Münsterberg.

In 1888, Hugo Münsterberg, a comparatively unknown young German psychologist, produced at the age of twenty-five a book, *Die Willenshandlung*, of which James thought highly, and to which he referred in the *Principles*. The famous experimental psychologist, G. E. Müller, however, gave the book a scathing review; whereupon James (who had never met Münsterberg) wrote him the following very characteristic letter:

Dear Dr Münsterberg, – I have just read Prof. G. E. Müller's review of you in the G.G.H., and find it in many respects so brutal that I am impelled to send you a word of 'consolation', if such a thing be possible. German polemics in general are not distinguished by mansuetude; but there is something peculiarly hideous in the business when an established authority like Müller, instead of administering fatherly and kindly admonition to a youngster like yourself, shows a malign pleasure in knocking him down and jumping up and down upon his body. All your merits he passes by parenthetically as *selbstverständlich*; your sins he enlarges upon with unction. Don't mind it! Don't be angry! Turn the other cheek! Make no ill-mannered reply! – and great will be your credit and reward! Answer by continuing your work and making it more and more irreproachable.

I can't myself agree in some of your theories. . . . But I find in you just what is lacking in this critique of Müller's – a sense for the perspective and proportion of things (so that, for instance, you *don't* make experiments and quote figures to the 100th decimal, where a coarse qualitative result is all that the question needs). Whose *theories* in Psychology have any *definitive* value to-day? No one's! Their only use is to sharpen further reflexion and observation. The man who throws out most new ideas and immediately seeks to subject them to experimental control is the most useful psychologist, in the present state of the science. No one has done this as yet as well as you. If you are only *flexible* towards your theories, and as ingenious in testing them hereafter as you have been hitherto, I will back you to beat the whole army of your critics before you are forty years old.[29]

Some two years later, the psychological laboratory at Harvard was enlarged and re-equipped. The laboratory had been founded by James, who had nursed it through its early stages, but experimental psychology had never attracted him,[30] and, now that its importance was increasing, he decided to look for someone who would take this branch of the work entirely off his hands. Münsterberg's name at once suggested itself ('he is the ablest experimental psychologist in Germany, allowance being made for the fact that he is only twenty-eight years old'); so, despite the fact that Münsterberg spoke little English (a handicap, James felt, that time would soon remove) James wrote to him 'sounding' him as to the possibility of his accepting the post if it were offered. Münsterberg returned a prompt affirmative by telegram, and a few months later James thankfully handed over the laboratory to his direction.

Münsterberg came to Harvard in 1892 – ten years after

29. LWJ, I, 312.

30. There is a well-known passage in the *Principles* in which James remarks that experimental psychology (which originated in Germany) 'could hardly have arisen in a country whose natives could be *bored. . . .* There is little of the grand style about these new prism, pendulum and chronograph philosophies' (P of P, I, 192–3). Later, in a letter to Flournoy, he wrote: 'The results that come from all this laboratory work seem to me to grow more and more disappointing and trivial. What is most needed is new ideas. For every man who has one of them, one may find a hundred who are willing to drudge patiently at some unimportant experiment' (LWJ, II, 54). Still later he wrote to Stumpf that 'the thought of psycho-physical experimentation, and altogether of brass-instrument and algebraic-formula psychology fills me with horror' (Perry, II, 195).

Royce, and just as James was due for another sabbatical year (this was the year – cf. p. 35 above – in which James so rashly took the children abroad). Royce, therefore, who was then Assistant Professor, was left in charge, with the newly-arrived young lecturer to help him. Royce kept James in touch with the affairs of the Department by letters, in one of which, after remarking that 'Cambridge without you is like toast unbuttered, like the heart without blood,' he continued 'Münsterberg is an immense success. His English is charming. The students love it as a mother her babe's first prattle. He fears them not, and they revere his wisdom the more, the more his speech is shattered. To me he is a great comfort, although, of course, no *Ersatz* for the aforesaid condition of my heart.'[31]

In its mixture of affection and polemic, the atmosphere of the Philosophy Department under James must have been very like that of the James household under Henry senior. Personally, Royce and James were devoted to one another, but intellectually they were at opposite poles. Royce was a Hegelian, and Hegel was James's philosophic *bête noire*. Royce believed in the Absolute, and in vast, deductive metaphysical systems, while James was an empiricist to the core. Their approach to philosophy was so different that it was obvious that they could never convince one another; but this was on the whole an advantage, since it meant that the discussion need never stop.

The flavour of this happily contentious relationship is well conveyed by the following letter from James to Royce. James was in Germany; he was having treatment for his heart, which he had strained while walking in the Adirondacks (cf. p. 55) and, in the intervals of treatment, incubating the Gifford Lectures which he was to give in Edinburgh the following year.

31. Perry, I, 803.

Beloved Royce, – Great was my, was *our* pleasure in receiving your long and delightful letter last night. Like the lioness in Aesop's fable, you give birth to one young one only in the year, but that one is a lion. I give birth mainly to guinea-pigs in the shape of postcards; but despite such diversities of epistolary expression, the heart of each of us is in the right place. I need not say, my dear old boy, how touched I am at your expressions of affection, or how it pleases me to hear that you have missed me. I too miss you profoundly. I do not find in the hotel waiters, chambermaids and bath-attendants with whom my lot is chiefly cast, that unique mixture of erudition, originality, profundity and vastness, and human wit and leisureliness, by accustoming me to which during all these years you have spoilt me for inferior kinds of intercourse. You are still the centre of my gaze, the pole of my mental magnet. When I write, 't is with one eye on the page, and one on you. When I compose my Gifford lectures mentally, 't is with the design exclusively of overthrowing your system, and ruining your peace. I lead a parasitic life upon you, for my highest flight of ambitious ideality is to become your conqueror, and go down into history as such, you and I rolled in one another's arms and silent (or rather loquacious still) in one last death-grapple of an embrace.[32]

After James's retirement from his Harvard professorship, a dinner was held to celebrate the completion and presentation of his portrait. At this dinner Royce made a speech, from which the following extracts are taken:

Nothing is more characteristic of Professor James's work as a teacher and as a thinker than is his chivalrous fondness for fair play in the warfare and in the co-operation of ideas and of ideals. ... Other men talk of liberty of thought: but few men have done more to secure liberty of thought for men who were in need of fair play and of a reasonable hearing than James has done. Now I suppose that it is altogether, or almost altogether, because of James's chivalry of soul that I myself first obtained that opportunity in life which results in my being here with you at all. . . .

Royce then told the story of his first meeting with James, continuing:

James . . . made out what my essential interests were at our first interview, accepted me, with all my imperfections, as one of those many souls who ought to be able to find themselves in their own way, gave a patient and willing ear to just my variety of philosophical experience, and used his influence from that time on, not to win me as a follower, but to give me my chance. It was upon his responsibility that I was later led to get my first opportunities here at Harvard. Whatever I am is in that sense due to him. . . .

Sometimes critical people have expressed this by saying that James has always been too fond of cranks, and that the cranks have loved him. Well, I am one of James's cranks. He was good to me, and I love him. The result of my own early contact with James was to make me for years very much his disciple. I am still in large part under his spell. If I contend with him sometimes, I suppose that it is he also who through his own free spirit has in great measure taught me this liberty. I know that for years I used to tremble at the thought that James might perhaps some day find reason to put me in my place by some one of those wonderful lightning-like epigrams, wherewith he was and is always able to characterize those opponents whose worldly position is such as to make them no longer in danger of not getting a fair hearing, and whose self-assurance has relieved him of the duty to secure for them a sympathetic attention. The time has passed, the lightning in question has often descended — never indeed on me as his friend, but often on my opinions — and has long since blasted, I hope, some at least of what is most combustible about my poor teachings. Yet I am so glad of the friendly words that still sustain me, that these occasional *segnende Blitze*, when incidentally they are sown over the earth where my opinions chance to be growing, only make me love better the cause that James . . . has so nobly served, the cause of fertilizing the human soil where our truth has to grow.[33]

After much goading from his long-suffering publishers, James finished writing the *Principles of Psychology* in the spring of 1890. He dispatched the last consignment of manuscript ('woodcuts and all') with the sensation of Christian dropping his burden; then, as he wrote to Mrs James:

> I came home very weary, and lit a fire, and had a delicious two hours all by myself, thinking of the big *étape* of my life which now lay behind me (I mean that infernal book done), and of the possibilities that the future yielded of reading and living and loving out from the shadow of that interminable black cloud. . . . At any rate, it does give me some comfort to think that I don't live *wholly* in projects, aspirations and phrases, but now and then have something done to show for all the fuss. The joke of it is that I, who have always considered myself a thing of glimpses, of discontinuity, of *aperçus*, with no power of doing a big job, suddenly realize at the *end* of this task that it is the biggest book on psychology in any language except Wundt's, Rosmini's and Daniel Greenleaf Thompson's! Still, if it burns up at the printing-office, I shan't much care, for I shan't ever write it again![34]

The book appeared in the autumn, and was an immediate and resounding success. The *Revue Philosophique* described it as '*une œuvre glorieuse*', and most reviewers agreed with Stanley Hall in regarding it as 'on the whole the best work [on this subject] in any language'. Adverse criticisms came from three main quarters: from those who (like Sully in the passages already quoted) felt that there

33. Perry, I, 779–80.
34. LWJ, I, 295.

was something a trifle unseemly in the brilliance of the style; from those who disliked the physiological approach and complained (as did C. S. Pierce) that the book was 'materialistic to the core'; and from those who criticized the somewhat unsystematic arrangement, and deplored James's tendency to prefer exciting speculation to the sober exposition of established fact. The most penetrating criticism of the latter kind came from Stanley Hall:

The author might be described as an *impressionist* in psychology. His portfolio contains sketches old and new, ethical, literary, scientific and metaphysical, some exquisite and charming in detail and even colour, others rough charcoal outlines, but all together stimulating and suggestive, and showing great industry and great versatility.... This is through and through a 'tendence' book. Its very inconsistencies and incoherencies not only reflect but greatly magnify all the unrest, distraction and conflicts of the present hour. The author is a veritable storm-bird, fascinated by problems most impossible of solution, and surest where specialists and experts in his own field are most in doubt, and finding it very hard to get up interest in the most important matters, if settled and agreed to, even to state them well.[35]

This criticism, though strongly worded, is not unjustified; but the defects of the book are outweighed by its surpassing merits. No other textbook published in the 'nineties has much chance of being read to-day by anyone except a student of the history of psychology, but the *Principles* is still widely read for its own sake.[36] One reason for this is that the book, though it is inevitably out of date on points of detail, is almost startlingly modern in its general approach. Most of the unsolved problems with which James was preoccupied – such as the relation between brain-processes and consciousness, or the physiology of the

35. Perry, II, 108–9.

36. A widely-used modern textbook – Cole's *General Psychology*, published in 1939 – contains thirteen index-references to the *Principles*.

learning process – are still unsolved, and still burning questions, to-day. Many later developments are fore-shadowed: James's attacks on Associationism, for example, at many points anticipated the *Gestalt* school, while his account of the processes of reasoning and creative thought was strikingly similar to that given thirty years later by Spearman (cf. pp. 130, 138-50). Also, unlike most psycho-logists of his time, James did not confine himself to the cognitive aspects of experience. He was interested in the emotions and motives of human beings, as well as in their perceptual and intellectual processes: and he anticipated present-day social psychology in his emphasis on the social factors which mould individual behaviour. Again, he fully realised the importance of contemporary investigations into such subjects as hypnotism, dissociation and subconscious memory – investigations which were either ignored or regarded as suspect by most academic psychologists of the day. Finally, and most fundamentally, he was years ahead of his time in his view that psychology, in so far as it 'belongs' with any other subject, 'belongs' with biology and physiology rather than with philosophy. As early as 1875, in a letter to the President of Harvard, James expressed the view that 'Psychology cannot be taught as a living science by anyone who has not a first-hand acquaint-ance with the facts of nervous physiology'. It was fifty years at least before academic opinion caught up with this view – if, indeed, it can be said to have caught up with it yet.

Many of the specific doctrines of the *Principles* have profoundly influenced the subsequent trend of psychology. Of these doctrines the most influential was probably that of the 'stream of consciousness', with all that it implied in the rejection of psychological atomism. Earlier psycho-logists had tended to talk of consciousness as though it were composed of discrete elements. But, as James pointed out, though it may sometimes be convenient to treat experience as consisting of separate ideas and sensations (just as it is convenient for certain purposes to treat a line as a series of points, or a river as a collection of drops), these divisions do not really exist in nature. They are 'mere arbitrary results of conceptual handling on our part'. Three facts about consciousness are repeatedly emphasized in the *Principles*: (i) consciousness is continuous, (ii) it includes the apprehension of relations as well as elements, of 'transitive' as well as 'substantive' states, and (iii) it has a fringe as well as a focus: though attention is focused on a centre, we are always aware of a vague and sliding stream of impressions and sensations at the periphery. The limitations of language make it difficult to give facts of this kind their due weight in describing our mental life; but James was peculiarly fitted to deal with this difficulty, since he had an exceptional power of fixing and crystallizing the most elusive and fugitive states of consciousness; as Perry says, 'he could see most cunningly out of the corner of his eye'. His introspective account of the experience of searching one's memory for a forgotten fact, for example (pp. 128-9), or his description of the 'revelation' experienced on coming round from nitrous oxide (pp. 210-11) show how successfully he fulfilled his declared intention of 'reinstating the vague and inarticulate to its proper place in our mental life' (cf. p. 97).

The theory with which James's name is most closely associated is still, probably, his theory of emotion – commonly known as the James-Lange theory, since it was put forward almost simultaneously by James and by the Danish physiologist, Lange. This theory reversed the usual assumption about cause and effect: it held that the emotion is the perception of certain bodily changes (such as quickened heart-beats, shallow breathing, trembling, etc.) and not (as is commonly believed) that the bodily changes take place as the result of the emotion. 'Common-sense says, we lose our fortune, are sorry and weep . . . we are insulted by a rival, are angry and strike; but the more rational statement is that we feel sorry because we cry, and angry because we strike.'[37] The theory aroused much interest and controversy in James's lifetime, but it is no longer a live issue, since it has now been conclusively refuted by the work of Sherrington, Cannon, and others.[38]

James was undoubtedly one of the greatest writers of his generation; hence discussion of the *Principles* tends to begin and end with its style. In one of his earliest published essays, written in his twenties, James referred to 'that imponderable superfluity, grace, without which no awakening of men's sympathies on a large scale can take place'. James himself possessed this quality in full measure. And he had not only grace, but the indispensable virtue of clarity.

There is a well-known saying about two golfers; the good golfer plays a difficult stroke and makes it look easy, while the bad golfer plays an easy stroke and makes it look difficult; and the saying has applications beyond the golf-course. Some writers and lecturers owe their reputation for profundity to the obscurity of their style rather than to the depth of their thought; even commonplace ideas will sound difficult if they are sufficiently enshrouded in verbiage. James, on the other hand, made difficult ideas clear by the infinite pains he took in their exposition. He

37. PBC, 375–6.
38. This is not to deny that emotions have physical causes. But modern research has shown that they are caused primarily by processes in the thalamic region of the brain, and that it is these same thalamic processes which give rise (via the autonomic nervous system) to the involuntary physical changes by which the emotion is accompanied.

was by no means an easy or rapid writer; he would doubtless have agreed with the author of *Hudibras* that 'easy
writing's damned hard reading'. Apropos of the *Principles*
he said in a letter to a friend, 'if there is aught of good in
the style, it is the result of ceaseless toil in re-writing.
Everything comes out wrong with me at first; but when
once objectified in a crude shape, I can torture and poke
and scrape and pat it till it offends me no more'.   In
another letter he replied to James Ward, who had evidently
congratulated him on his ability to 'dash off' popular
lectures, 'I don't "dash off" that kind of stuff any more
than any other kind, but forge it all with blood and sweat,
and groans and lamentations to heaven, and vows that I
will never start to write anything again'.

The clarity of James's style was heightened by his
exceptional gift for apt analogy and metaphor. His metaphors (*pace* Sully) do not merely dazzle; they illuminate.
He never descended to the trick of some modern popular
writers, of trying to atone for the obscurity of their
exposition by sprinkling the pages with more or less irrelevant jokes. He made his points in a witty and memorable
way, which is a very different thing.

The two volumes of the *Principles* contain nearly 1,400
pages, and it soon became obvious that the length of the
book was the one serious objection to its use by University
students. Accordingly, two years after its publication,
James, at the instigation of his publishers, produced an
abridgment – officially entitled the *Briefer Course*,[39] but
commonly known to students as the 'Jimmy', to distinguish
it from the parent work, the 'James'. To quote from the
preface:

39. The English edition is entitled *Textbook of Psychology*.

In preparing the following abridgment of my larger work, the *Principles of Psychology*, my chief aim has been to make it more directly available for class-room use. For this purpose I have omitted several whole chapters and rewritten others. I have left out all the polemical and historical matter, all the metaphysical discussions and purely speculative passages, most of the quotations, all the book-references, and (I trust) all the impertinences, of the larger work, leaving to the teacher the task of orally restoring as much of this material as may seem to him good. ... Knowing how ignorant the average student is of physiology, I have added brief chapters on the various senses. ... About two-fifths of the volume is either new or rewritten, the rest is 'scissors and paste'.[40]

For the private ear of his publisher he put the matter somewhat differently:

My dear Holt, – I expect to send you within ten days the MS. of my *Briefer Course*, boiled down to possibly 400 pages. By adding some twaddle about the senses, by leaving out all polemics and history, all bibliography and experimental details, all metaphysical subtleties and digressions, all quotations, all humour and pathos, all *interest* in short, and by blackening the tops of all the paragraphs, I think I have produced a tome of pedagogic classic which will enrich both you and me, if not the student's mind.[41]

James's motives for producing the 'Jimmy' were frankly financial, and his view of it was always a trifle jaundiced. Actually, it is a first-rate introductory textbook, and the chapters containing the 'twaddle about the senses' are models of straight exposition which go far to redress the lack of balance (as between unsolved problems and 'matters settled and agreed to') of which Hall had complained in the *Principles*. Financially, the book more than fulfilled James's hopes, for it became, and remained for many years, the most widely sold textbook on psychology in the English language.

After the publication of the *Principles* and the *Briefer Course*, James felt that he had written himself out on the subject of psychology. For the next ten years, his psychological writings were confined to reviews and articles, and his main interests turned more and more towards philosophy. In 1902, however, he made a triumphal re-entry into the psychological field with *The Varieties of Religious Experience*. This book was the result of an invitation to lecture in Edinburgh under the auspices of the Gifford Trust – a Trust established by Lord Gifford for the provision of annual lecture-courses on Natural Religion in the Scottish Universities. Many eminent men have been Gifford lecturers, among them Lord Haldane, A. J. Balfour and James Ward.

James's approach to his subject was objective and psychological; his aim, as he said in the first lecture, was to give 'a descriptive survey of man's religious propensities'. But as the course continued a thesis gradually emerged. This thesis is perhaps most clearly summarized in a letter to Miss Frances Morse, in which James said, 'The problem I have set myself is a hard one: *first*, to defend . . . "experience" against "philosophy" as being the real backbone of the world's religious life . . . and *second*, to make the hearer or reader believe, what I myself invincibly do believe, that, although all the special manifestations of religion may have been absurd (I mean its creeds and theories), yet the life of it as a whole is mankind's most important function.'[42] The topic was one which suited James's genius perfectly, and the *Varieties* (described by Perry as 'a monument of erudition and

42. Perry, II, 326–7.

insight') is by common consent his greatest book after the *Principles*.

Apart from the *Varieties*, James produced no major psychological work in the latter part of his life. To psychologists, the diversion of his interests towards philosophy must inevitably be a matter for regret; and, quite apart from professional bias, the fact is undeniable that James the philosopher was not in the same class as James the psychologist. James the psychologist, for all his high spirits and speculative boldness, had a thoroughly responsible and professional attitude towards his subject. He 'spoke with authority' – an authority derived, in large part, from his firm basis of physiological and biological knowledge. As he himself said, in a passage from his Diary which has already been quoted, and which would serve admirably as a motto for the *Principles*, 'The concrete facts in which a biologist's responsibilities lie form a fixed basis from which to aspire as much as he pleases to the mastery of universal questions when the gallant mood is on him'.[43] But James the philosopher had no such 'fixed basis', for he never got over his youthful dislike of formal logic, and almost made a virtue of his aversion from it. Consequently, though he could never fail to be stimulating, James the philosopher was at best little more than a brilliant and slightly irresponsible amateur.

The philosophical theory (or, as some would say, aberration) with which James was most closely connected, is known as *pragmatism*. Pragmatism is the spiritual ancestor of logical positivism. The core of the doctrine is, that beliefs do not, as most people would suppose, work because they are true, but are true in that they work. (James had a curious fondness for these paradoxical reversals – compare his theory that we are frightened

43. LWJ, I, 171.

because we run, and angry because we strike). The doctrine of pragmatism was first adumbrated in *The Will to Believe*,[44] published in 1897, and in an article entitled "Philosophical Conceptions and Practical Results' published a year later. In 1907 it reached its final and least defensible stage in *Pragmatism* – a book for which James himself had a surprising affection, but which most critics agree in regarding as his least satisfactory work.

No extracts from *Pragmatism*, or any other of James's purely philosophical writings, are included in the selections that follow. But since the pragmatist theory made many distinguished converts, it may be well to trace it briefly through its various stages. *The Will to Believe* consists largely of a spirited defence of empirical as against 'absolutist' methods in philosophy. James profoundly distrusted all those metaphysical systems (of which Hegelianism is the prototype) which claim to reach certain truth by *a priori* reasoning. Philosophy, in his view, could advance only by adopting the inductive and empirical method of the natural sciences – that is, by abandoning the claim to logical certainty, and by advancing from one provisional working hypothesis to another. James further argued, as against contemporary agnostics like Clifford and T. H. Huxley, that we have as much right to adopt working hypotheses in the religious as in the scientific sphere. In 1873 James defined the essence of the religious hypothesis as 'the affirmation that all is *not* vanity'; and in *The Will to Believe* he argued that, though this hypothesis can be neither proved nor disproved, we are not (*pace* Clifford) committing an intellectual crime if we base our lives on the assumption of its truth. Similarly with more specific

44. 'The Will to Believe' was originally delivered as an address to the Philosophical Clubs of Yale and Brown Universities. It was subsequently published, together with nine other papers, in a volume whose full title is *The Will to Believe and other Essays in Popular Philosophy*.

hypotheses, as that there is a moral order in the universe, or a spiritual reality underlying the material world. If by 'backing' these hypotheses we can live happier and more effective lives, there is no reason why we should not do so; provided, of course, that we realize that they *are* hypotheses, and do not persecute those who reject them.

In developing this thesis, James scored a number of points against those simple-minded rationalists who suppose that all their beliefs are based on adequate intellectual evidence. Indeed, in his emphasis on the part played by non-rational factors in forming our beliefs, and by rationalization in justifying them after the event, James to some extent anticipated the psycho-analysts. Consider, for example, the following passage from *The Will to Believe:*

Here in this room, we all of us believe in molecules and the conservation of energy, in democracy and necessary progress, in Protestant Christianity and the duty of fighting for 'the doctrine of the immortal Monroe', all for no reasons worthy of the name. We see into these matters with no more inner clearness, and probably with much less, than any disbeliever in them might possess. His unconventionality would probably have some grounds to show for its conclusions; but for us, not insight, but the *prestige* of the opinions, is what makes the spark shoot from them and light up our sleeping magazines of faith. Our reason is quite satisfied, in nine hundred and ninety-nine cases out of every thousand of us, if it can find a few arguments that will do to recite in case our credulity is criticised by someone else. Our faith is faith in someone else's faith.[45]

In *Pragmatism*, published ten years later, James carried the argument several stages further. The essential thesis of *The Will to Believe* (with which few people would quarrel) is that we are often justified in adopting a belief as a working hypothesis, even though its truth cannot be conclusively proved. In *Pragmatism*, however, James purported to *define* truth in terms of 'working': a 'true' belief was said to mean, by definition, a belief that 'works', or a belief that it is 'advantageous' to hold.

There are two fundamental objections to this proposed definition. In the first place, the meaning of the term 'works' has been tacitly, and illicitly, extended. In his earlier formulations, when he spoke of a belief 'working', James used the term in the normal scientific sense, in which a hypothesis 'works' (roughly speaking) if it explains many facts and conflicts with none. But in *Pragmatism* beliefs are said to 'work' if the holding of them is conducive to virtue or (with reservations) to happiness. Clearly this is an entirely different sense of 'working'; and much of the intellectual discomfort felt by readers of *Pragmatism* is due to the fact that the two senses are never clearly distinguished.

A second and even more fundamental objection is that the proposed definition involves a vicious circle. 'To hold a belief' is equivalent to 'to regard a belief as true': so if we substitute the second expression for the first, the definition becomes 'A true belief is a belief that it is advantageous to regard as true' – which is clearly circular. (A correspondent, Benjamin Blood, put what is essentially the same point when he said, 'When you say "pragmatism is the truth about truth", the first truth is different from the second'.) Such was James's intolerance of formal logic, however, that he could never be got to see that there was any force in this objection; any tendency on the part of his critics to dwell on it he dismissed as 'mere pettifogging and logic-chopping'. Indeed, it is doubtful whether he ever fully understood the nature of a definition, in the logical sense; for in many passages where he purports to be *defining* truth in terms of 'advantage', all he is really doing is putting forward 'advantage' as a *criterion* of the truth of a belief.[46] But even as a criterion, 'advantage' is not completely valid. We can no doubt say, in a broad sense, that it is advantageous to believe what is true, just as we can say, in the same broad sense, that foods that are palatable are wholesome. But there are enough individual exceptions to both principles to make it extremely rash to use advantage as a criterion of truth, or palatability of wholesomeness. To take but one of many possible examples, it is sometimes disadvantageous for a patient to hold a true belief about the nature of his illness.

However, despite (or perhaps because of) its logical weaknesses, Pragmatism had an immense popular success. The book *Pragmatism* is based on a course of lectures which James delivered at the Lowell Institute in Boston in 1906, and repeated at Columbia University, New York, a year later. The New York lectures, in particular, created something of a *furore:* the audience numbered over a thousand, and James described this week of his life as 'certainly the high tide of my existence, so far as energizing and being "recognized" were concerned'.

46. The distinction between a definition and a criterion may be illustrated as follows. If we say 'a spinster is an unmarried woman' or 'a bungalow is a one-storied house' we are giving genuine definitions of the terms 'spinster' and 'bungalow'. But if we say 'spinsters do not wear wedding-rings' we are not defining the meaning of the term 'spinster', but stating a *criterion* by which spinsters may be recognized.

If a proposed definition contains in it the term to be defined, the definition is circular. Thus it would clearly be circular to define a snob as one who is always complaining that other people are snobbish. But if the statement that snobs are always complaining (etc.) is in fact true, and if it is also true that no non-snobs exhibit this tendency, then the tendency in question will constitute a valid *criterion* of snobbery. To put the point more formally, if Q is a valid criterion of P this implies (i) that 'P' and 'Q' are not identical in meaning, and (ii) that all P's have Q and that no *non-P*'s have it. Thus, though it is circular to *define* a true belief as a belief which it is advantageous to regard as true, there is no purely logical objection to using 'advantageous (etc.)' as a *criterion* of truth.

The lecture, rather than the treatise, was the mode of expression that James found most congenial. All his most successful writings, from the *Principles* onwards, were based on the spoken word. After the publication of the *Principles*, James devoted an increasing amount of time to popular and semi-popular lecturing[47] – impelled thereto partly by public demand, partly by personal inclination, and partly by the financial needs of his family. The time and energy consumed in this way were considerable, and what was a gain to the general public was a loss to philosophy: James never fulfilled his ambition of producing a major philosophical work on the scale of the *Principles*. But whether on balance posterity has gained or lost, is an open question. There have been many better philosophers than James, but no-one with quite his unique combination of psychological insight, common-sense, wit and articulateness; and it might well be argued that no philosophical system that James was capable of producing would have been worth the sacrifice of *Talks to Teachers*, *Memories and Studies*, and the other brilliant books in which he carried the fruits of his years of research and teaching into the market-place.

The history of James's last years can be recounted briefly. Among his favourite recreations were walking and climbing in the mountains around his country home in New Hampshire; and on one such expedition, in June 1899, he lost his way, and 'converted what was to have been a "walk" into a thirteen-hours' scramble'. His heart had already shown signs of weakness, and the result was an irreparable valvular lesion. The Gifford lectures, which he was to have delivered in Edinburgh in the

47. Most of these lectures were published in James's lifetime. Others were collected in the posthumous *Memories and Studies* and *Collected Essays and Reviews*.

following spring, had to be postponed, and James spent the next two years in a state of semi-invalidism in Europe. It seemed for a time as though his active career was ended, and he made several offers to resign his Harvard professorship. These offers, however, the University authorities firmly refused, and their optimism was justified; by the spring of 1901, James's condition had greatly improved. He was able to give the postponed Gifford lectures, which had undoubtedly gained in value from their prolonged incubation, and in the autumn he resumed his Harvard teaching with a half-course on 'The Psychological Elements of the Religious Life'. He continued to lecture at Harvard, though on a part-time basis, until 1907, and he contrived also to do a considerable amount of outside lecturing, culminating in the strenuous week in which he was lionized in New York as the founder of pragmatism.

When James finally retired from University work, in January 1907, it was with the intention of passing the remainder of his days (as he wrote to Henry) 'in a different manner, contemplatively namely, and with leisure and simplification for the one remaining thing, which is to report in one book, at least, such impressions as my own intellect has received from the universe'. This object, as we have seen, he never fully achieved. His most ambitious philosophical work, *Some Problems of Philosophy*, was unfinished at his death. This book was originally planned as a University textbook, and it differs from most of James's work in being written for readers rather than for an audience. Here, if anywhere, James carried out his intention of 'abandoning the squashy popular-lecture style', and writing something 'serious, systematic and syllogistic'. It is, in Perry's phrase, 'the most technical and carefully-reasoned 'of all his works; but it is one of the least read.

A less ambitious, but in some ways far more successful book was *A Pluralistic Universe*, published in 1909. This is written in James's habitual lecturing style, though it could not be described as popular; it consists of Hibbert lectures on 'The Present Situation in Philosophy', delivered at Manchester College, Oxford. As a philosophic writer James had one supreme merit; he could expound the views of other philosophers, often far more clearly than they could expound them themselves: and in *A Pluralistic Universe* this gift had full scope, since nearly half the book is devoted to exposition of the theories of Hegel, Fechner and Bergson. It was characteristic of James that he considered it impossible to understand or criticize an author without putting oneself at the centre of his vision by an act of imaginative insight. He was impatient of what he called 'the whole Ph.D. industry' of scoring debating points against a writer by convicting him of verbal inconsistency. Such criticism he described as 'crawling over the thing like a myopic ant over a building, tumbling into every microscopic crack or fissure, finding nothing but inconsistencies, and never suspecting that a centre exists.'[48] James thoroughly lived up to his own principles in this matter, with the result that, despite his well-known antipathy to Hegel, the third chapter of *A Pluralistic Universe* contains what is probably the best brief account of the Hegelian *Weltanschauung* ever given.[49] *A Pluralistic Universe* shows James the philosopher at his best. It is in many respects a brilliant book, and in the opinion of

48. *A Pluralistic Universe*, p. 263.

49. Many readers must have shared the experience of Ernst Mach, who wrote to James, 'I have constantly tried to read Hegel, supposing that I would find profound ideas in him, but I have never succeeded in arriving at a good understanding of him. . . . Through your third lecture a first understanding of Hegel seems to dawn upon me. For this illumination I am grateful' (Perry, II, 594).

Palmer (James's predecessor in the Chair of Philosophy at Harvard) it deserved to restore James to 'the high position from which that horrid volume on *Pragmatism*' had tended to pull him down.

But James's philosophic system was destined, in his own phrase, to remain like 'a bridge begun and stopped in the middle of an arch'. In 1910 his heart again began to give serious trouble, and once again he visited Europe for rest and treatment. But the panacea was no longer effective. His condition deteriorated, and by August he had only one desire left — to return home. With Mrs James and his brother Henry, he embarked at Liverpool for the last time; and after an anxious and painful journey, the three reached Chocorua, James's New Hampshire home, on 19 August. There James, in the words of his son, 'sank into a chair beside the fire, sobbing "it's so good to be home".' He died a week later.

James's life provides a striking illustration of the Freudian doctrine that the foundations of character are laid in childhood. The domestic atmosphere in which he was brought up, with its combination of emotional security and intellectual adventure, left a stamp on each member of the James family; but on none more clearly than on William, whose whole approach to life, and the whole tone of whose published writings, reflect the influence of those early, formative years. Few people in their lifetime can have inspired more affection than James. His magnanimity, his capacity for self-criticism, and his complete lack of pettiness; his individual and unusual blend of robustness and subtlety, of catholicity and discrimination, of wit and 'high seriousness', made him a uniquely attractive figure. As James Ward wrote, in a letter to James sent shortly before his death, 'Yours, my dear friend, has been a successful life, and surely it has been a happy one, for I know of no-one more universally beloved. I, at least, never heard an ill word of you from anyone'.

APPENDIX: A NOTE ON WILLIAM AND HENRY JAMES

EVEN a short account of James's life would be incomplete without some further reference to his relations with his brother Henry. The two men differed as much in character as in literary style, but the bond between members of the James family was stronger than all temperamental divergences. Henry, as is well known, settled permanently in England in his early forties, and thereafter, in the manner of some expatriates, became more English than the English. William had no great sympathy with this development, but the affection between the brothers was not weakened; they corresponded regularly when they were apart, and never failed to make contact on William's frequent visits to Europe. After one such visit William wrote to his sister Alice 'Harry has been delightful ... and beneath all the accretions of years and the world, is still the same dear, innocent old Harry of our youth. His anglicisms are but "protective resemblances" – he's really, I won't say a Yankee, but a native of the James family, and has no other country.'[50] The temptation to rag Henry, however, was at times irresistible. One suspects that William's American accent became more marked in Henry's presence; and his letters to his brother were apt to contain such remarks as 'give me a human race with some *guts* to them, no matter if they do belch at you now and then' – an observation which to poor Henry's ears must have sounded almost obscene. Furthermore, no amount of fraternal affection could reconcile William to Henry's 'third manner' as a novelist. Writing to Henry in 1905 apropos of *The Golden Bowl* he said:

The method of narration by interminable elaboration of suggestive reference (I don't know what to call it, but you know what I mean) goes agin the grain of all my own impulses in writing; and yet in spite of it all, there is a brilliancy and cleanness of effect, and in this book especially a high-toned social atmosphere that are unique and extraordinary. Your methods and my ideals seem the reverse, the one of the other — and yet I have to admit your extreme success in this book. But why won't you, just to please Brother, sit down and write a new book, with no twilight or mustiness in the plot, with great vigour and decisiveness in the action, no fencing in the dialogue, no psychological commentaries, and absolute straightness in the style? Publish it in my name, I will acknowledge it, and give you half the proceeds. Seriously, I wish you *would*, for you *can;* and I should think it would tempt you, to embark on a 'fourth manner'.[51]

Henry received this helpful suggestion a trifle coldly:

I mean (in response to what you write me of your having read the *Golden Bowl*) to try to produce some uncanny form of thing in fiction, that will gratify you, as Brother — but let me say, dear William, that I shall greatly be humiliated if you *do* like it, and thereby lump it, in your affection, with things, of the current age, that I have heard you express admiration for and that I would sooner descend to a dishonoured grave than have written.[51]

With the publication of *The American Scene*, however, William returned unruffled to the attack:

You know how opposed your whole 'third manner' of execution is to the literary ideals which animate my crude and Orson-like breast, mine being to say a thing in one sentence as straight and explicit as it can be made, and then to drop it forever; yours being to avoid naming it straight, but by dint of breathing and sighing all round and round it, to arouse in the reader who may have had a similar perception already (Heaven help him if he hasn't!) the illusion of a solid object, made (like the 'ghost' at the Polytechnic) wholly out of impalpable materials, air, and the prismatic interference of light, ingeniously focused by mirrors upon empty space. But you *do* it, that's the queerness! ... But it's the rummest method for one to employ systematically as you do nowadays; and you employ it at your peril. In this crowded and hurried reading age, pages that require such close attention remain unread and neglected. ... And so I say now, give us *one* thing in your older directer manner, just to show that, in spite of your paradoxical success in this unheard-of method, you *can* still write according to accepted canons.[52]

Henry's reply is not recorded!

Finally, H. G. Wells in his *Autobiography* describes a meeting with the James brothers which shows each in a characteristic light. William was staying with Henry at the latter's home in Rye, and Wells had called with a car to fetch William, who was to spend the day with him at Sandgate. He found the brothers engaged in heated argument in the garden.

[Henry] had lost his calm; he was terribly unnerved. He appealed to me, to me of all people, to adjudicate on what was and what was not permissible behaviour in England. William was arguing about it in an indisputably American accent, with an indecently naked reasonableness. William had none of Henry's passionate regard for the polish upon the surfaces of life, and he was immensely excited by the fact that in the little Rye inn, which had its garden just over the high brick wall of the garden of Lamb House, G. K. Chesterton was staying. William James had corresponded with our vast contemporary and he sorely wanted to see him. So with a scandalous directness he had put the gardener's ladder against that ripe red wall, clambered up and peeped over. Henry had caught him at it.

52. LWJ, II, 277–8.

It was the sort of thing that isn't done. It was most emphatically the sort of thing that isn't done. . . . Henry had instructed the gardener to put away that ladder, and William was looking thoroughly naughty about it. To Henry's manifest relief I carried William off, and in the road just outside the town we ran against the Chestertons. . . . William got his coveted impression.

THE PRINCIPLES OF
PSYCHOLOGY

AND THE

BRIEFER COURSE

The Principles of Psychology
AND THE
Briefer Course

INTRODUCTORY: BODY AND MIND

The definition of Psychology may be best given in the words of Professor Ladd, as the *description and explanation of states of consciousness as such.* By states of consciousness are meant such things as sensations, desires, emotions, cognitions, reasonings, decisions, volitions, and the like. Their 'explanation' must of course include the study of their causes, conditions, and immediate consequences, so far as these can be ascertained.

Mental facts cannot be properly studied apart from the physical environment of which they take cognizance. The great fault of the older rational psychology was to set up the soul as an absolute spiritual being with certain faculties of its own by which the several activities of remembering, imagining, reasoning, willing, etc., were explained, almost without reference to the peculiarities of the world with which these activities deal. But the richer insight of modern days perceives that our inner faculties are *adapted* in advance to the features of the world in which we dwell, adapted, I mean, so as to secure our safety and prosperity in its midst. Not only are our capacities for forming new habits, for remembering sequences, and for abstracting general properties from things and associating their usual consequences with them, exactly the faculties needed for steering us in this world of mixed variety and uniformity, but our emotions and instincts are adapted to very special features of that world. In the main, if a phenomenon is important for our welfare, it interests and excites us the first time we come into its presence. Dangerous things fill us with involuntary fear; poisonous things with distaste; indispensable things with appetite. Mind and world in short have been evolved together, and in consequence are something of a mutual fit. The special interactions between the outer order and the order of consciousness, by which this harmony, such as it is, may in the course of time have come about, have been made the subject of many evolutionary speculations, which, though they cannot so far be said to be conclusive, have at least refreshed and enriched the whole subject, and brought all sorts of new questions to the light.

The chief result of all this more modern view is the gradually growing conviction that *mental life is primarily teleological;* that is to say, that our various ways of feeling and thinking have grown to be what they are because of their utility in shaping our *reactions* on the outer world. On the whole, few recent formulas have done more service in psychology than the Spencerian one that the essence of mental life and bodily life are one, namely, 'the adjustment of inner to outer relations'. The adjustment is to immediately present objects in lower animals and in infants. It is to objects more and more remote in time and space, and inferred by means of more and more complex and exact processes of reasoning, when the grade of mental development grows more advanced. . . .

It was said above that the 'conditions' of states of consciousness must be studied. *The immediate condition of a state of consciousness is an activity of some sort in the cerebral hemispheres.* This proposition is supported by so many pathological facts, and laid by physiologists at the base of so many of their reasonings, that to the medically educated mind it seems almost axiomatic. It would be hard, however, to give any short and peremptory proof of the unconditional dependence of mental action upon neural change. That a general and usual amount of dependence exists cannot possibly be ignored. One has only to consider how quickly consciousness may be (so far as we know) abolished by a blow on the head, by rapid loss of blood, by an epileptic discharge, by a full dose of alcohol, opium, ether, or nitrous oxide – or how easily it may be altered in quality by a smaller dose of any of these agents or of others, or by a fever, – to see how at the mercy of bodily happenings our spirit is. A little stoppage of the gall-duct, a swallow of cathartic medicine, a cup of strong coffee at the proper moment, will entirely overturn for the time a man's views of life. . . . Whether a man shall be a hero or a coward is a matter of his temporary 'nerves'. In many kinds of insanity, though by no means in all, distinct alterations of the brain-tissue have been found. Destruction of certain definite portions of the cerebral hemispheres involves losses of memory and of acquired motor faculty of quite determinate sorts. . . . Taking all such facts together, the simple and radical conception dawns upon the mind that mental action may be uniformly and absolutely a function of brain-action, varying as the latter varies, and being to the brain-action as effect to cause.[1]

This conception is the 'working hypothesis' which underlies all the 'physiological psychology' of recent years, and it will be the working hypothesis of this book. Taken thus absolutely, it may possibly be too sweeping a statement of what in reality is only a partial truth. But the only way to make sure of its unsatisfactoriness is to apply it seriously to every possible case that can turn up. To work an hypothesis 'for all it is worth' is the real, and often the only, way to prove

1. [Editor's footnote.] These arguments have been greatly strengthened since James's day by such developments as pre-frontal leucotomy – a brain operation which may completely transform the personality – and by recent discoveries about the way in which temperament and character are affected by the ductless gland secretions.

its insufficiency. I shall therefore assume without scruple at the outset that the uniform correlation of brain-states with mind-states is a law of nature. The interpretation of the law in detail will best show where its facilities and where its difficulties lie. To some readers such an assumption will seem like the most unjustifiable *a priori* materialism. In one sense it doubtless is materialism: it puts the Higher at the mercy of the Lower. But although we affirm that the *coming to pass* of thought is a consequence of mechanical laws, – for, according to another 'working hypothesis', that namely of physiology, the laws of brain-action are at bottom mechanical laws, – we do not in the least explain the *nature* of thought by affirming this dependence, and in that latter sense our proposition is not materialism. The authors who most unconditionally affirm the dependence of our thoughts on our brain to be a fact are often the loudest to insist that the fact is inexplicable,[2] and that the intimate essence of consciousness can never be rationally accounted for by any material cause. It will doubtless take several generations of psychologists to test the hypothesis of dependence with anything like minuteness. The books which postulate it will be to some extent on conjectural ground. But the student will remember that the Sciences constantly have to take these risks, and habitually advance by zig-zagging from one absolute formula to another which corrects it by going too far the other way. At present Psychology is on the materialistic tack, and ought in the interests of ultimate success to be allowed full headway even by those who are certain she will never fetch the port without putting down the helm once more.

2. [Editor's footnote.] As James says in his final chapter, 'Something happens when to a certain brain-state a certain "sciousness" corresponds. A genuine glimpse into what it is would be *the* scientific achievement, before which all past achievements would pale' (P B C., 468).

Up to this point, James seems to be defending the 'automaton theory', which caused him such mental distress in the early part of his life (cf. pp. 30–1). The theory is now commonly known as epipheno-menalism, since it holds that mental processes are epiphenomena or by-products of brain-processes. The classical exposition of this theory was given by T. H. Huxley in an address ('On the Hypothesis that Animals are Automata, and its History') to the British Association at Belfast in 1874.[3]

In fact, however, James was not a thorough-going epiphenomenalist. Though he accepted as a working hypothesis the principle that every state of conscious-ness is caused by a brain-state (a principle which is accepted, tacitly or explicitly, by all physiological psychologists to-day), James did not accept Huxley's corollary that states of mind have therefore no causal effectiveness. He held that conscious states, though they owe their existence to brain-processes, can nevertheless react, once they are in existence, in such a way as 'to further or to dampen the processes to which they are due'. In a later chapter James expounds this view, which is a compromise between epiphenomenalism and the common-sense or inter-actionist hypothesis.

[The champions of the automaton theory], finding that reflex and semi-automatic acts may, notwithstanding their appropriateness, take place with an unconsciousness appar-ently complete, maintain that the appropriateness even of the higher voluntary actions connected with the hemi-spheres owes nothing to the fact that consciousness attends

3. Published in *Method and Results* (Vol. I of T. H. Huxley's Collected Essays), 1893.

them. They are, according to these writers, results of physiological mechanism pure and simple.

To comprehend completely this latter doctrine one should apply it to examples. The movements of our tongues and pens, the flashings of our eyes in conversation, are of course events of a physiological order, and as such their causal antecedents may be exclusively mechanical. If we knew thoroughly the nervous system of Shakespeare, and as thoroughly all his environing conditions, we should be able, according to the theory of automatism, to show why at a given period of his life his hand came to trace on certain sheets of paper those crabbed little black marks which we for shortness' sake call the manuscript of Hamlet. We should understand the rationale of every erasure and alteration therein, and we should understand all this without in the slightest degree acknowledging the existence of the thoughts in Shakespeare's mind. The words and sentences would be taken, not as signs of anything beyond themselves, but as little outward facts, pure and simple. In like manner, the automaton-theory affirms, we might exhaustively write the biography of those two hundred pounds, more or less, of warmish albuminoid matter called Martin Luther, without ever implying that it felt.

But, on the other hand, nothing in all this could prevent us from giving an equally complete account of either Luther's or Shakespeare's spiritual history, an account in which every gleam of thought and emotion should find its place. The mind-history would run alongside of the body-history of each man, and each point in the one would correspond to, but not react upon, a point in the other. So the melody floats from the harp-string, but neither checks nor quickens its vibrations; so the shadow runs alongside the pedestrian, but in no way influences his steps.

As a mere *conception*, and so long as we confine our view

to the nervous centres themselves, few things are more seductive than this radically mechanical theory of their action. And yet our consciousness *is there*, and has in all probability been evolved, like all other functions, for a use — it is to the highest degree improbable *a priori* that it should have no use. Its use *seems* to be that of *selection*; but to select, it must be efficacious. States of consciousness which feel right are held fast to; those which feel wrong are checked. If the 'holding' and the 'checking' of the conscious states severally mean also the efficacious reinforcing or inhibiting of the correlated neural processes, then it would seem as if the presence of the states of mind might help to steer the nervous system and keep it in the path which to the consciousness seemed best. Now on the average what seems best to consciousness is really best for the creature. It is a well-known fact that pleasures are generally associated with beneficial, pains with detrimental, experiences. All the fundamental vital processes illustrate this law. Starvation; suffocation; privation of food, drink, and sleep; work when exhausted; burns, wounds, inflammation; the effects of poison, are as disagreeable as filling the hungry stomach, enjoying rest and sleep after fatigue, exercise after rest, and a sound skin and unbroken bones at all times, are pleasant.

Probability and circumstantial evidence thus run dead against the theory that our actions are *purely* mechanical in their causation. From the point of view of descriptive Psychology (even though we be bound to assume, as on p. 67, that all our feelings have brain-processes for their condition of existence, and can be remotely traced in every instance to currents coming from the outer world) we have no clear reason to doubt that the feelings may react so as to further or to dampen the processes to which they are due. I shall therefore not hesitate in the course of this book to use the language of common-sense. I shall talk as if consciousness kept actively pressing the nerve-centres in the direction of its own ends, and was no mere impotent and paralytic spectator of life's game.

The body-mind relationship was one of those 'problems impossible of solution' which continued to fascinate James throughout his life. He returned to it in his more philosophical writings, where the views he expressed often seem considerably less 'material-istic' than even the qualified epiphenomenalism that he expounds above. The gap, however, is to a large extent bridged by one of his less-known works, the Ingersoll lecture on *Human Immortality*. James there argued that, though there is overwhelming evidence for the functional dependence of mind on brain, such dependence does not necessarily imply that the brain *generates* consciousness: it may merely *transmit* it. Behind the material world there may be a 'continuum of cosmic consciousness', which is transmitted through material brains in a sense analogous to that in which light is transmitted through coloured glass. Differ-ences in personality, intelligence, etc., between different individuals, will thus depend on differences in the transmitting media. Elsewhere, James sug-gested that there may be, not a single cosmic con-sciousness, but many. The concluding chapters of *The Varieties of Religious Experience* can be fully understood only in the light of this hypothesis.

The theory was never fully worked out, and does not appear to have aroused much interest in James's lifetime. But it may now be necessary to take it more seriously, in view of the accumulating evidence for extra-sensory perception and other forms of paranormal cognition. These phenomena *may* not be incompatible with epiphenomenalism, but they can certainly be more easily reconciled with a transmission hypothesis.

HABIT

MANY besides psychologists are familiar with 'James on Habit' — the most famous Chapter of the *Principles*, and one of the most effective lay sermons that can ever have been delivered in a lecture-room. The Chapter has special value to-day, as an antidote to the current misconception that psychology depreciates the will, and encourages a weak-kneed and fatalistic acceptance of one's own deficiencies.

Its Importance for Psychology. There remains a condition of general neural activity so important as to deserve a chapter by itself — I refer to the aptitude of the nerve-centres, especially of the hemispheres, for acquiring habits. *An acquired habit, from the physiological point of view, is nothing but a new pathway of discharge formed in the brain, by which certain incoming currents ever after tend to escape.* That is the thesis of this chapter; and we shall see in the later and more psychological chapters that such functions as the association of ideas, perception, memory, reasoning, the education of the will, etc., etc., can best be understood as results of the formation *de novo* of just such pathways of discharge.

Habit has a physical basis. The moment one tries to define what habit is, one is led to the fundamental properties of matter. [Habits, in the widest sense, are due to the plasticity of materials to outward agents.] The philosophy of habit is thus, in the first instance, a chapter in physics rather than in physiology or psychology. That it is at bottom a physical principle, is admitted by all good recent writers on the subject. They call attention to analogues of acquired habits exhibited by dead matter. Thus, M. Léon Dumont writes:

'Every one knows how a garment, after having been worn a certain time, clings to the shape of the body better than when it was new; there has been a change in the tissue, and this change is a new habit of cohesion. A lock works better after being used some time; at the outset more force was required to overcome certain roughness in the mechanism. The overcoming of their resistance is a pheno-menon of habituation. It costs less trouble to fold a paper when it has been folded already; ... and just so in the nervous system the impressions of outer objects fashion for themselves more and more appropriate paths, and these vital phenomena recur under similar excitements from without, when they have been interrupted a certain time.'

Not in the nervous system alone. A scar anywhere is a *locus minoris resistentiæ*, more liable to be abraded, inflamed, to suffer pain and cold, than are the neighbouring parts. A sprained ankle, a dislocated arm, are in danger of being sprained or dislocated again; joints that have once been attacked by rheumatism or gout, mucous membranes that have been the seat of catarrh, are with each fresh recur-rence more prone to a relapse. . . .

Habits are due to pathways through the nerve-centres. If habits are due to the plasticity of materials to outward agents, we can immediately see to what outward influences, if to any, the brain-matter is plastic. Not to mechanical pressures, not to thermal changes, not to any of the forces to which all the other organs of our body are exposed; for Nature has so blanketed and wrapped the brain about that the only impressions that can be made upon it are through the blood, on the one hand, and the sensory nerve-roots, on the other; and it is to the infinitely attenuated currents that pour in through these latter channels that the hemispherical cortex shows itself to be so peculiarly susceptible. The currents, once in, must find a way out. In getting out they leave their traces in the paths which they take. The only thing they *can* do, in short, is to deepen old paths or to make new ones; and the whole plasticity of the brain sums itself up in two words when we call it an organ in which currents pouring in from the sense-organs make with extreme facility paths which do not easily disappear. For, of course, a simple habit, like every other nervous event – the habit of snuffling, for example, or of putting one's hands into one's pockets, or of biting one's nails – is, mechanically, nothing but a reflex discharge; and its anatomical substratum must be a path in the system. The most complex habits, as we shall presently see more fully, are, from the same point of view, nothing but *concatenated* discharges in the nerve-centres, due to the presence there of systems of reflex paths, so organized as to wake each other up successively – the impression produced by one muscular contraction serving as a stimulus to provoke the next, until a final impression inhibits the process and closes the chain. . . .

The physical basis of learning and habit-formation is still one of the major unsolved problems of psychology. James's suggested explanation is certainly oversimplified; psychologists do not now talk confidently about the deepening of nerve-paths, but, cautiously and provisionally, about the setting-up of patterns of electro-chemical activity in the brain. But though James's physiological theory is out of date, this does not affect the value of his practical conclusions, since these do not depend on any *particular* theory of the physical basis of habit. All that they imply is that habit has *some* physiological basis – or, more specifically, that every experience involves some infinitesimal modification (no matter what) in the nervous system.

Practical Effects of Habit. First, habit simplifies our movements, makes them accurate, and diminishes fatigue.

Man is born with a tendency to do more things than he has ready-made arrangements for in his nerve-centres. Most of the performances of other animals are automatic. But in him the number of them is so enormous that most of them must be the fruit of painful study. If practice did not make perfect, nor habit economize the expense of nervous and muscular energy, he would be in a sorry plight. . . .

Secondly, *habit diminishes the conscious attention with which our acts are performed.*

One may state this abstractly thus: If an act require for its execution a chain, *A, B, C, D, E, F, G*, etc., of successive nervous events, then in the first performance of the action the conscious will must choose each of these events from a number of wrong alternatives that tend to present themselves; but habit soon brings it about that each event calls up its own appropriate successor without any alternative offering itself, and without any reference to the conscious will, until at last the whole chain, *A, B, C, D, E, F, G*, rattles itself off as soon as *A* occurs, just as if *A* and the rest of the chain were fused into a continuous stream. Whilst we are learning to walk, to ride, to swim, skate, fence, write, play, or sing, we interrupt ourselves at every step by unnecessary movements and false notes. When

we are proficients, on the contrary, the results follow not
only with the very minimum of muscular action requisite
to bring them forth, but they follow from a single instantaneous 'cue'. The marksman sees the bird, and, before he
knows it, he has aimed and shot. A gleam in his adversary's
eye, a momentary pressure from his rapier, and the fencer
finds that he has instantly made the right parry and return.
A glance at the musical hieroglyphics, and the pianist's
fingers have rippled through a shower of notes. And not
only is it the right thing at the right time that we thus
involuntarily do, but the wrong thing also, if it be an
habitual thing. Who is there that has never wound up his
watch on taking off his waistcoat in the daytime, or taken
his latch-key out on arriving at the door-step of a friend?
Persons in going to their bedroom to dress for dinner have
been known to take off one garment after another and
finally to get into bed, merely because that was the
habitual issue of the first few movements when performed
at a later hour. We all have a definite routine manner of
performing certain daily offices connected with the toilet,
with the opening and shutting of familiar cupboards, and
the like. But our higher thought-centres know hardly
anything about the matter. Few men can tell off-hand
which sock, shoe, or trousers-leg they put on first. They
must first mentally rehearse the act; and even that is often
insufficient – the act must be *performed*. So of the questions,
Which valve of the shutters opens first? Which way does
my door swing? etc. I cannot *tell* the answer; yet my *hand*
never makes a mistake. No one can *describe* the order in
which he brushes his hair or teeth; yet it is likely that the
order is a pretty fixed one in all of us. . . .

*Ethical and Pedagogical Importance of the Principle of
Habit.* 'Habit a second nature! Habit is ten times nature',
the Duke of Wellington is said to have exclaimed; and the

degree to which this is true no one probably can appreciate as well as one who is a veteran soldier himself. The daily drill and the years of discipline end by fashioning a man completely over again, as to most of the possibilities of his conduct.

'There is a story', says Professor Huxley, 'which is credible enough, though it may not be true, of a practical joker who, seeing a discharged veteran carrying home his dinner, suddenly called out, "Attention!" whereupon the man instantly brought his hands down, and lost his mutton and potatoes in the gutter. The drill had been thorough, and its effects had become embodied in the man's nervous structure. . . .'

Habit is thus the enormous fly-wheel of society, its most precious conservative agent. It alone is what keeps us all within the bounds of ordinance, and saves the children of fortune from the envious uprisings of the poor. It alone prevents the hardest and most repulsive walks of life from being deserted by those brought up to tread therein. It keeps the fisherman and the deck-hand at sea through the winter; it holds the miner in his darkness, and nails the countryman to his log-cabin and his lonely farm through all the months of snow; it protects us from invasion by the natives of the desert and the frozen zone. It dooms us all to fight out the battle of life upon the lines of our nurture or our early choice, and to make the best of a pursuit that disagrees, because there is no other for which we are fitted, and it is too late to begin again. It keeps different social strata from mixing. Already at the age of twenty-five you see the professional mannerism settling down on the young commercial traveller, on the young doctor, on the young minister, on the young counsellor-at-law. You see the little lines of cleavage running through the character, the tricks of thought, the prejudices, the ways of the 'shop', in a word, from which the man can by-and-by no more escape than his coat-sleeve can suddenly fall into a new set of folds. On the whole, it is best he should not escape. It is well for the world that in most of us, by the age of thirty, the character has set like plaster, and will never soften again.

If the period between twenty and thirty is the critical one in the formation of intellectual and professional habits, the period below twenty is more important still for the fixing of *personal* habits, properly so called, such as vocalization and pronunciation, gesture, motion, and address. Hardly ever is a language learned after twenty spoken without a foreign accent; hardly ever can a youth transferred to the society of his betters unlearn the nasality and other vices of speech bred in him by the associations of his growing years. Hardly ever, indeed, no matter how much money there be in his pocket, can he even learn to *dress* like a gentleman-born. The merchants offer their wares as eagerly to him as to the veriest 'swell', but he simply *cannot* buy the right things. An invisible law, as strong as gravitation, keeps him within his orbit, arrayed this year as he was the last; and how his better-clad acquaintances contrive to get the things they wear will be for him a mystery till his dying day.

The great thing, then, in all education, is to *make our nervous system our ally instead of our enemy*. It is to fund and capitalize our acquisitions, and live at ease upon the interest of the fund. *For this we must make automatic and habitual, as early as possible, as many useful actions as we can*, and guard against the growing into ways that are likely to be disadvantageous to us, as we should guard against the plague. The more of the details of our daily life we can hand over to the effortless custody of automatism, the more our higher powers of mind will be set free for their own proper work. There is no more miserable human being than one in whom nothing is habitual but indecision, and for whom the lighting of every cigar, the drinking of every cup, the time of rising and going to bed every day, and the beginning of every bit of work, are subjects of express volitional deliberation. Full half the time of such a man goes to the deciding, or regretting, of matters which ought to be so ingrained in him as practically not to exist for his consciousness at all. If there be such daily duties not yet ingrained in any one of my readers, let him begin this very hour to set the matter right.

In Professor Bain's chapter on 'The Moral Habits' there are some admirable practical remarks laid down. Two great maxims emerge from his treatment. The first is that in the acquisition of a new habit, or the leaving off of an old one, we must take care to *launch ourselves with as strong and decided an initiative as possible.* Accumulate all the possible circumstances which shall re-enforce the right motives; put yourself assiduously in conditions that encourage the new way; make engagements incompatible with the old; take a public pledge, if the case allows; in short, envelop your resolution with every aid you know. This will give your new beginning such a momentum that the temptation to break down will not occur as soon as it otherwise might; and every day during which a break-down is postponed adds to the chances of its not occurring at all.

The second maxim is: *Never suffer an exception to occur till the new habit is securely rooted in your life.* Each lapse is like the letting fall of a ball of string which one is carefully winding up; a single slip undoes more than a great many turns will wind again. *Continuity* of training is the great means of making the nervous system act infallibly right. . . .

The question of 'tapering-off', in abandoning such habits as drink and opium-indulgence comes in here, and is a question about which experts differ within certain limits, and in regard to what may be best for an individual case. In the main, however, all expert opinion would agree that abrupt acquisition of the new habit is the best way, *if there be a real possibility of carrying it out.* We must be careful not to give the will so stiff a task as to insure its defeat at the very outset; but, *provided one can stand it*, a sharp period of suffering, and then a free time, is the best thing to aim at, whether in giving up a habit like that of opium, or in simply changing one's hours of rising or of work. It is surprising how soon a desire will die of inanition if it be *never* fed. ...

A third maxim may be added to the preceding pair : *Seize the very first possible opportunity to act on every resolution you make, and on every emotional prompting you may experience in the direction of the habits you aspire to gain.* It is not in the moment of their forming, but in the moment of their producing *motor effects*, that resolves and aspirations communicate the new 'set' to the brain. . . .

No matter how full a reservoir of *maxims* one may possess, and no matter how good one's *sentiments* may be, if one have not taken advantage of every concrete opportunity to *act*, one's character may remain entirely unaffected for the better. With mere good intentions, hell is proverbially paved. And this is an obvious consequence of the principles we have laid down. A 'character', as J. S. Mill says, 'is a completely fashioned will'; and a will, in the sense in which he means it, is an aggregate of tendencies to act in a firm and prompt and definite way upon all the principal emergencies of life. A tendency to act only becomes effectively ingrained in us in proportion to the uninterrupted frequency with which the actions actually occur, and the brain 'grows' to their use. When a resolve or a fine glow of feeling is allowed to evaporate without bearing practical fruit it is worse than a chance lost; it works so as positively to hinder future resolutions and emotions from taking the normal path of discharge. There is no more contemptible type of human character than that of the nerveless sentimentalist and dreamer, who spends his life in a weltering sea of sensibility and emotion, but who never does a manly concrete deed. Rousseau, inflaming all the mothers of France, by his eloquence, to follow Nature and nurse their babies themselves, while he sends his own children to the foundling hospital, is the classical example of what I mean. But every one of us in his measure, whenever, after glowing for an abstractly formulated Good, he practically ignores some actual case, among the squalid 'other particulars' of which that same Good lurks disguised, treads straight on Rousseau's path. All Goods are disguised by the vulgarity of their concomitants, in this work-a-day world; but woe to him who can only recognize them when he thinks them in their pure and abstract form! The habit of excessive novel-reading and theatre-going will produce true monsters in this line. The weeping of the Russian lady over the fictitious personages in the play, while her coachman is freezing to death on his seat outside, is the sort of thing that everywhere happens on a less glaring scale. Even the habit of excessive indulgence in music, for those who are neither performers themselves nor musically gifted enough to take it in a purely intellectual way, has probably a relaxing effect upon the character. One becomes filled with emotions which habitually pass without prompting to any deed, and so the inertly sentimental condition is kept up. The remedy would be, never to suffer one's self to have an emotion at a concert, without expressing it afterwards in *some* active

way. Let the expression be the least thing in the world —
speaking genially to one's grandmother, or giving up one's
seat in a horse-car, if nothing more heroic offers — but let
it not fail to take place.

These latter cases make us aware that it is not simply
particular lines of discharge, but also *general forms* of
discharge, that seem to be grooved out by habit in the
brain. Just as, if we let our emotions evaporate, they get
into a way of evaporating; so there is reason to suppose
that if we often flinch from making an effort, before we
know it the effort-making capacity will be gone; and that,
if we suffer the wandering of our attention, presently it
will wander all the time. Attention and effort are, as we
shall see later, but two names for the same psychic fact.
To what brain processes they correspond we do not know.
The strongest reason for believing that they do depend on
brain-processes at all, and are not pure acts of the spirit, is
just this fact, that they seem in some degree subject to the
law of habit, which is a material law. As a final practical
maxim, relative to these habits of the will, we may, then,
offer something like this: *Keep the faculty of effort alive
in you by a little gratuitous exercise every day*. That is,
be systematically ascetic or heroic in little unnecessary
points, do every day or two something for no other reason
than that you would rather not do it, so that when the
hour of dire need draws nigh, it may find you not unnerved
and untrained to stand the test. Asceticism of this sort is
like the insurance which a man pays on his house and
goods. The tax does him no good at the time, and possibly
may never bring him a return. But if the fire *does* come,
his having paid it will be his salvation from ruin. So with
the man who has daily inured himself to habits of concentrated attention, energetic volition, and self-denial in
unnecessary things. He will stand like a tower when every-

thing rocks around him, and when his softer fellow-mortals are winnowed like chaff in the blast.

The physiological study of mental conditions is thus the most powerful ally of hortatory ethics. . . . Could the young but realize how soon they will become mere walking bundles of habits, they would give more heed to their conduct while in the plastic state. We are spinning our own fates, good or evil, and never to be undone. Every smallest stroke of virtue or of vice leaves its never so little scar. The drunken Rip Van Winkle, in Jefferson's play, excuses himself for every fresh dereliction by saying, 'I won't count this time!' Well! he may not count it, and a kind Heaven may not count it: but it is being counted none the less. Down among his nerve-cells and fibres the molecules are counting it, registering and storing it up to be used against him when the next temptation comes. Nothing we ever do is, in strict scientific literalness, wiped out. Of course this has its good side as well as its bad one. As we become permanent drunkards by so many separate drinks, so we become saints in the moral, and authorities and experts in the practical and scientific spheres, by so many separate acts and hours of work. Let no youth have any anxiety about the upshot of his education, whatever the line of it may be. If he keep faithfully busy each hour of the working day, he may safely leave the final result to itself. He can with perfect certainty count on waking up some fine morning, to find himself one of the competent ones of his generation, in whatever pursuit he may have singled out. Silently, between all the details of his business, the *power of judging* in all that class of matter will have built itself up within him as a possession that will never pass away. Young people should know this truth in advance. The ignorance of it has probably engendered more discouragement and faint-heartedness in youths embarking on arduous careers than all other causes put together.

THE STREAM OF CONSCIOUSNESS

IF the chapter on 'Habit' is the best known in the *Principles*, the chapter on 'The Stream of Consciousness' has most profoundly influenced the subsequent development of psychology. Cf. Introduction, pp. 44–5.

The order of our study must be analytic. We are now prepared to begin the introspective study of the adult consciousness itself. Most books adopt the so-called synthetic method. Starting with 'simple ideas of sensation' and regarding these as so many atoms, they proceed to build up the higher states of mind out of their 'association', 'integration', or 'fusion', as houses are built by the agglutination of bricks. This has the didactic advantages which the synthetic method usually has. But it commits one beforehand to the very questionable theory that our higher states of consciousness are compounds of units; and instead of starting with what the reader directly knows, namely his total concrete states of mind, it starts with a set of supposed 'simple ideas' with which he has no immediate acquaintance at all, and concerning whose alleged interactions he is much at the mercy of any plausible phrase. On every ground, then, the method of advancing from the simple to the compound exposes us to illusion. All pedants and abstractionists will naturally hate to abandon it. But a student who loves the fulness of human nature will prefer to follow the 'analytic' method, and to begin with the most concrete facts, those with which he has a daily acquaintance in his own inner life. The analytic method will discover in due time the elementary parts, if such exist, without danger of precipitate assumption. . . .

The Fundamental Fact. The first and foremost concrete fact which every one will affirm to belong to his inner experience is the fact that *consciousness of some sort goes on.* 'States of mind' succeed each other in him. If we could say in English 'it thinks', as we say 'it rains' or 'it blows', we should be stating the fact most simply and with the minimum of assumption. As we cannot, we must simply say that *thought goes on.*

Four Characters in Consciousness. How does it go on? We notice immediately four important characters in the process, of which it shall be the duty of the present chapter to treat in a general way:

(1) Every 'state' tends to be part of a personal consciousness.

(2) Within each personal consciousness states are always changing.

(3) Each personal consciousness is sensibly continuous.

(4) It is interested in some parts of its object to the exclusion of others, and welcomes or rejects – *chooses* from among them, in a word – all the while.

In considering these four points successively, we shall have to plunge *in medias res* as regards our nomenclature and use psychological terms which can only be adequately defined in later chapters of the book. But every one knows what the terms mean in a rough way; and it is only in a rough way that we are now to take them. This chapter is like a painter's first charcoal sketch upon his canvas, in which no niceties appear.

(1) When I say *every 'state' or 'thought' is part of a personal consciousness,* 'personal consciousness' is one of the terms in question. Its meaning we know so long as no one asks us to define it, but to give an accurate account of it is

the most difficult of philosophic tasks. This task we must confront in the next chapter; here a preliminary word will suffice.

In this room – this lecture-room, say – there are a multitude of thoughts, yours and mine, some of which cohere mutually, and some not. They are as little each-for-itself and reciprocally independent as they are all-belonging-together. They are neither: no one of them is separate, but each belongs with certain others and with none beside. My thought belongs with *my* other thoughts, and your thought with *your* other thoughts. Whether anywhere in the room there be a *mere* thought, which is nobody's thought, we have no means of ascertaining, for we have no experience of its like. The only states of consciousness that we naturally deal with are found in personal consciousnesses, minds, selves, concrete particular I's and you's. . . .

(2) *Consciousness is in constant change.* I do not mean by this to say that no one state of mind has any duration – even if true, that would be hard to establish. What I wish to lay stress on is this, that *no state once gone can recur and be identical with what it was before.* Now we are seeing, now hearing; now reasoning, now willing; now recollecting, now expecting; now loving, now hating; and in a hundred other ways we know our minds to be alternately engaged. But all these are complex states, it may be said, produced by combination of simpler ones; – do not the simpler ones follow a different law? Are not the *sensations* which we get from the same object, for example, always the same? Does not the same piano-key, struck with the same force, make us hear in the same way? Does not the same grass give us the same feeling of green, the same sky the same feeling of blue, and do we not get the same olfactory sensation no matter how many times we put our

nose to the same flask of cologne? It seems a piece of metaphysical sophistry to suggest that we do not; and yet a close attention to the matter shows that *there is no proof that an incoming current ever gives us just the same bodily sensation twice.*

What is got twice is the same OBJECT. We hear the same *note* over and over again; we see the same *quality* of green, or smell the same objective perfume, or experience the same *species* of pain. The realities, concrete and abstract, physical and ideal, whose permanent existence we believe in, seem to be constantly coming up again before our thought, and lead us, in our carelessness, to suppose that our 'ideas' of them are the same ideas. When we come, some time later, to the chapter on Perception, we shall see how inveterate is our habit of simply using our sensible impressions as stepping-stones to pass over to the recognition of the realities whose presence they reveal. The grass out of the window now looks to me of the same green in the sun as in the shade, and yet a painter would have to paint one part of it dark brown, another part bright yellow, to give its real sensational effect. We take no heed, as a rule, of the different way in which the same things look and sound and smell at different distances and under different circumstances. The sameness of the *things* is what we are concerned to ascertain; and any sensations that assure us of that will probably be considered in a rough way to be the same with each other. . . .

Our sensibility is altering all the time, so that the same object cannot easily give us the same sensation over again. We feel things differently accordingly as we are sleepy or awake, hungry or full, fresh or tired; differently at night and in the morning, differently in summer and in winter; and above all, differently in childhood, manhood, and old age. And yet we never doubt that our feelings reveal the same world, with the same sensible qualities and the same sensible things occupying it. . . .

To these indirect presumptions that our sensations, following the mutations of our capacity for feeling, are always undergoing an essential change, must be added another presumption, based on what must happen in the brain. Every sensation corresponds to some cerebral action. For an identical sensation to recur it would have to occur the second time *in an unmodified brain.* But as this, strictly speaking, is a physiological impossibility, so is an unmodified feeling an impossibility; for to every brain-modification, however small, we suppose that there must correspond a change of equal amount in the consciousness which the brain subserves. . . .

The proposition that no two 'ideas' are ever exactly the same, is more important theoretically than it at first sight seems. For it makes it already impossible for us to follow obediently in the footprints of either the Lockian or the Herbartian school, schools which have had almost unlimited influence in Germany and among ourselves. No doubt it is often *convenient* to formulate the mental facts in an atomistic sort of way, and to treat the higher states of consciousness as if they were all built out of unchanging simple ideas which 'pass and turn again'. It is convenient often to treat curves as if they were composed of small straight lines, and electricity and nerve-force as if they were fluids. But in the one case as in the other we must never forget that we are talking symbolically, and that there is nothing in nature to answer to our words. *A permanently existing 'Idea' which makes its appearance before the footlights of consciousness at periodical intervals is as mythological an entity as the Jack of Spades.*

(3) *Within each personal consciousness, thought is sensibly continuous.* I can only define 'continuous' as that which

is without breach, crack, or division. The only breaches that can well be conceived to occur within the limits of a single mind would either be *interruptions*, *time*-gaps during which the consciousness went out; or they would be breaks in the content of the thought, so abrupt that what followed had no connection whatever with what went before. The proposition that consciousness feels continuous, means two things:

(*a*) That even where there is a time-gap the consciousness after it feels as if it belonged together with the consciousness before it, as another part of the same self;

(*b*) That the changes from one moment to another in the quality of the consciousness are never absolutely abrupt.

The case of the time-gaps, as the simplest, shall be taken first.

(*a*) When Paul and Peter wake up in the same bed, and recognize that they have been asleep, each one of them mentally reaches back and makes connection with but *one* of the two streams of thought which were broken by the sleeping hours. As the current of an electrode buried in the ground unerringly finds its way to its own similarly buried mate, across no matter how much intervening earth; so Peter's present instantly finds out Peter's past, and never by mistake knits itself on to that of Paul. Paul's thought in turn is as little liable to go astray. The past thought of Peter is appropriated by the present Peter alone. He may have a *knowledge*, and a correct one too, of what Paul's last drowsy states of mind were as he sank into sleep, but it is an entirely different sort of knowledge from that which he has of his own last states. He *remembers* his own states, whilst he only *conceives* Paul's. Remembrance is like direct feeling; its object is suffused with a warmth and intimacy to which no object of mere conception ever attains. This quality of warmth and intimacy and immediacy is what

Peter's *present* thought also possesses for itself. . . . What the qualities called warmth and intimacy may in themselves be will have to be matter for future consideration. But whatever past states appear with those qualities must be admitted to receive the greeting of the present mental state, to be owned by it, and accepted as belonging together with it in a common self. This community of self is what the time-gap cannot break in twain. . . .

Consciousness, then, does not appear to itself chopped up in bits. Such words as 'chain' or 'train' do not describe it fitly as it presents itself in the first instance. It is nothing jointed; it flows. A 'river' or a 'stream' are the metaphors by which it is most naturally described. *In talking of it hereafter, let us call it the stream of thought, of consciousness, or of subjective life.*

(*b*) But now there appears, even within the limits of the same self, and between thoughts all of which alike have this same sense of belonging together, a kind of jointing and separateness among the parts, of which this statement seems to take no account. I refer to the breaks that are produced by sudden *contrasts in the quality* of the successive segments of the stream of thought. If the words 'chain' and 'train' had no natural fitness in them, how came such words to be used at all? Does not a loud explosion rend the consciousness upon which it abruptly breaks, in twain? Does not every sudden shock, appearance of a new object, or change in a sensation, create a real interruption, sensibly felt as such, which cuts the conscious stream across at the moment at which it appears? . . .

This objection is based [largely] on a confusion . . . between the thoughts themselves, taken as subjective facts, and the things of which they are aware. . . . The things are discrete and discontinuous; they do pass before us in a chain or train, making often explosive appearances and rending each other in twain. But their comings and goings and contrasts no more break the flow of the thought that thinks them than they break the time and space in which they lie. A silence may be broken by a thunder-clap, and we may be so stunned and confused for a moment by the shock as to give no instant account to ourselves of what has happened. But that very confusion is a mental state, and a state that passes us straight over from the silence to the sound. The transition between the thought of one object and the thought of another is no more a break in the *thought* than a joint in a bamboo is a break in the wood. It is a part of the *consciousness* as much as the joint is a part of the *bamboo*. . . .

'Substantive' and 'Transitive' States of Mind. When we take a general view of the wonderful stream of our consciousness, what strikes us first is the different pace of its parts. Like a bird's life, it seems to be an alternation of flights and perchings. The rhythm of language expresses this, where every thought is expressed in a sentence, and every sentence closed by a period. The resting-places are usually occupied by sensorial imaginations of some sort, whose peculiarity is that they can be held before the mind for an indefinite time, and contemplated without changing; the places of flight are filled with thoughts of relations, static or dynamic, that for the most part obtain between the matters contemplated in the periods of comparative rest.

Let us call the resting-places the 'substantive parts', and the places of flight the 'transitive parts', of the stream of thought. It then appears that our thinking tends at all times towards some other substantive part than the one from which it has just been dislodged. And we may say that the main use of the transitive parts is to lead us from one substantive conclusion to another.

Now it is very difficult, introspectively, to see the tran-

sitive parts for what they really are. If they are but flights
to a conclusion, stopping them to look at them before the
conclusion is reached is really annihilating them. Whilst if
we wait till the conclusion *be* reached, it so exceeds them
in vigour and stability that it quite eclipses and swallows
them up in its glare. Let anyone try to cut a thought across
in the middle and get a look at its section, and he will see
how difficult the introspective observation of the transitive
tracts is. The rush of the thought is so headlong that it
almost always brings us up at the conclusion before we can
arrest it. Or if our purpose is nimble enough and we do
arrest it, it ceases forthwith to be itself. As a snowflake
crystal caught in the warm hand is no longer a crystal but
a drop, so, instead of catching the feeling of relation moving
to its term, we find we have caught some substantive
thing, usually the last word we were pronouncing, statically
taken, and with its function, tendency, and particular
meaning in the sentence quite evaporated. The attempt at
introspective analysis in these cases is in fact like seizing a
spinning top to catch its motion, or trying to turn up the
gas quickly enough to see how the darkness looks. And the
challenge to *produce* these transitive states of consciousness,
which is sure to be thrown by doubting psychologists at
anyone who contends for their existence, is as unfair as
Zeno's treatment of the advocates of motion, when, asking
them to point out in what place an arrow *is* when it moves,
he argues the falsity of their thesis from their inability to
make to so preposterous a question an immediate reply.

The results of this introspective difficulty are baleful.
If to hold fast and observe the transitive parts of thought's
stream be so hard, then the great blunder to which all
schools are liable must be the failure to register them, and
the undue emphasizing of the more substantive parts of the
stream. Now the blunder has historically worked in two

ways. One set of thinkers have been led by it to *Sensationalism*. Unable to lay their hands on any substantive feelings corresponding to the innumerable relations and forms of connection between the sensible things of the world, finding no *named* mental states mirroring such relations, they have for the most part denied that any such states exist; and many of them, like Hume, have gone on to deny the reality of most relations *out* of the mind as well as in it. Simple substantive 'ideas', sensations and their copies, juxtaposed like dominoes in a game, but really separate, everything else verbal illusion, — such is the upshot of this view. The *Intellectualists*, on the other hand, unable to give up the reality of relations *extra mentem*, but equally unable to point to any distinct substantive feelings in which they were known, have made the same admission that such feelings do not exist. But they have drawn an opposite conclusion. The relations must be known, they say, in something that is no feeling, no mental 'state', continuous and consubstantial with the subjective tissue out of which sensations and other substantive conditions of consciousness are made. They must be known by something that lies on an entirely different plane, by an *actus purus* of Thought, Intellect, or Reason, all written with capitals and considered to mean something unutterably superior to any passing perishing fact of sensibility whatever.

But from our point of view both Intellectualists and Sensationalists are wrong. If there be such things as feelings at all, *then so surely as relations between objects exist* in rerum naturâ, *so surely, and more surely, do feelings exist to which these relations are known*. There is not a conjunction or a preposition, and hardly an adverbial phrase, syntactic form, or inflection of voice, in human speech, that does not express some shading or other of relation which we at some moment actually feel to exist between the large objects of our thought. If we speak objectively, it is the real relations that appear revealed; if we speak subjectively, it is the stream of consciousness that matches each of them by an inward colouring of its own. In either case the relations are numberless, and no existing language is capable of doing justice to all their shades. . . .

Consider once again the analogy of the brain. We believe the brain to be an organ whose internal equilibrium is always in a state of change – the change affecting every part. . . . But if consciousness corresponds to the fact of rearrangement itself, why, if the rearrangement stop not, should the consciousness ever cease? And if a lingering rearrangement brings with it one kind of consciousness, why should not a swift rearrangement bring another kind of consciousness as peculiar as the rearrangement itself?

The object before the mind always has a 'Fringe'. There are other unnamed modifications of consciousness just as important as the transitive states, and just as cognitive as they. Examples will show what I mean.

Suppose three successive persons say to us: 'Wait!' 'Hark!' 'Look!' Our consciousness is thrown into three quite different attitudes of expectancy, although no definite object is before it in any one of the three cases. Probably no one will deny here the existence of a real conscious affection, a sense of the direction from which an impression is about to come, although no positive impression is yet there. Meanwhile we have no names for the psychoses [4] in question but the names hark, look, and wait.

Suppose we try to recall a forgotten name. The state of our consciousness is peculiar. There is a gap therein; but no mere gap. It is a gap that is intensely active. A sort of

---

4. [Editor's footnote.] As used by James, this term has no pathological implications. A 'psychosis' means simply 'a state of mind'.

wraith of the name is in it, beckoning us in a given direction, making us at moments tingle with the sense of our closeness, and then letting us sink back without the longed-for term. If wrong names are proposed to us, this singularly definite gap acts immediately so as to negate them. They do not fit into its mould. And the gap of one word does not feel like the gap of another, all empty of content as both might seem necessarily to be when described as gaps. When I vainly try to recall the name of Spalding, my consciousness is far removed from what it is when I vainly try to recall the name of Bowles. Here some ingenious persons will say: 'How *can* the two consciousnesses be different when the terms which might make them different are not there? All that is there, so long as the effort to recall is vain, is the bare effort itself. How should that differ in the two cases? You are making it seem to differ by prematurely filling it out with the different names, though these, by the hypothesis, have not yet come. Stick to the two efforts as they are, without naming them after facts not yet existent, and you'll be quite unable to designate any point in which they differ.' Designate, truly enough. We can only designate the difference by borrowing the names of objects not yet in the mind. Which is to say that our psychological vocabulary is wholly inadequate to name the differences that exist, even such strong differences as these. But namelessness is compatible with existence. . . . There are innumerable consciousnesses of *want*, no one of which taken in itself has a name, but all different from each other. Such a feeling of want is *toto coelo* other than a want of feeling: it is an intense feeling. The rhythm of a lost word may be there without a sound to clothe it; or the evanescent sense of something which is the initial vowel or consonant may mock us fitfully, without growing more distinct. Every one must know the tantalizing effect of the blank rhythm of some forgotten verse, restlessly dancing in one's mind, striving to be filled out with words.

What is that first instantaneous glimpse of some one's meaning which we have, when in vulgar phrase we say we 'twig' it? Surely an altogether specific affection of our mind. And has the reader never asked himself what kind of a mental fact is his *intention of saying a thing* before he has said it? It is an entirely definite intention, distinct from all other intentions, an absolutely distinct state of consciousness, therefore; and yet how much of it consists of definite sensorial images, either of words or of things? Hardly anything! Linger, and the words and things come into the mind; the anticipatory intention, the divination is there no more. But as the words that replace it arrive, it welcomes them successively and calls them right if they agree with it, it rejects them and calls them wrong if they do not. The intention *to-say-so-and-so* is the only name it can receive. One may admit that a good third of our psychic life consists in these rapid premonitory perspective views of schemes of thought not yet articulate. . . .

It is, the reader will see, the reinstatement of the vague and inarticulate to its proper place in our mental life which I am so anxious to press on the attention. Mr Galton and Professor Huxley have, as we shall see in the chapter on Imagination, made one step in advance in exploding the ridiculous theory of Hume and Berkeley that we can have no images but of perfectly definite things. Another is made if we overthrow the equally ridiculous notion that, whilst simple objective qualities are revealed to our knowledge in 'states of consciousness', relations are not. But these reforms are not half sweeping and radical enough. What must be admitted is that the definite images of traditional psychology form but the very smallest part of our minds as they actually live. The traditional psychology talks like one who should say a river consists of nothing but pailsful, spoonsful, quartpotsful, barrelsful, and other moulded forms of water. Even were the pails and the pots all actually standing in the stream, still between them the free water would continue to flow. It is just this free water of consciousness that psychologists resolutely overlook. Every definite image in the mind is steeped and dyed in the free water that flows round it. With it goes the sense of its relations, near and remote, the dying echo of whence it came to us, the dawning sense of whither it is to lead. The significance, the value, of the image is all in this halo or penumbra that surrounds and escorts it, – or rather that is fused into one with it and has become bone of its bone and flesh of its flesh; leaving it, it is true, an image of the same *thing* it was before, but making it an image of that thing newly taken and freshly understood.

Let us call the consciousness of this halo of relations around the image by the name of 'psychic overtone' or 'fringe'.

Cerebral Conditions of the 'Fringe'. Nothing is easier than to symbolize these facts in terms of brain-action. Just as the echo of the *whence*, the sense of the starting point of our thought, is probably due to the dying excitement of processes but a moment since vividly aroused; so the sense of the whither, the foretaste of the terminus, must be due to the waxing excitement of tracts or processes whose psychical correlative will a moment hence be the vividly present feature of our thought. . . . It is just like 'overtones' in music: they are not separately heard by the ear; they blend with the fundamental note, and suffuse it, and alter it; and even so do the waxing and waning brain-processes at every moment blend with and suffuse and alter the psychic effect of the processes which are at their culminating point. . . .

(4) The last peculiarity to which attention is to be

drawn in this first rough description of thought's stream is that —

Consciousness is always interested more in one part of its object than in another, and welcomes and rejects, or chooses, all the while it thinks.

The phenomena of selective attention and of deliberative will are of course patent examples of this choosing activity. But few of us are aware how incessantly it is at work in operations not ordinarily called by these names. Accentuation and Emphasis are present in every perception we have . . .

But we do far more than emphasize things, and unite some, and keep others apart. We actually *ignore* most of the things before us. . . . We notice only those sensations which are signs to us of *things* which happen practically or æsthetically to interest us, to which we therefore give substantive names, and which we exalt to this exclusive status of independence and dignity. But in itself, apart from my interest, a particular dust-wreath on a windy day is just as much of an individual *thing*, and just as much or as little deserves an individual name, as my own body does. . . .

Next, in a world of objects thus individualized by our mind's selective industry, what is called our 'experience' is almost entirely determined by our habits of attention. A thing may be present to a man a hundred times, but if he persistently fails to notice it, it cannot be said to enter into his experience. Let four men make a tour in Europe. One will bring home only picturesque impressions — costumes and colours, parks and views and works of architecture, pictures and statues. To another all this will be non-existent; and distances and prices, populations and drainage-arrangements, door- and window-fastenings, and other useful statistics will take their place. A third will give a rich account of the theatres, restaurants, and public halls, and naught beside; whilst the fourth will perhaps have been so wrapped in his own subjective broodings as to be able to tell little more than a few names of places through which he passed. Each has selected, out of the same mass of presented objects, those which suited his private interest and has made his experience thereby. . . .

Taking human experience in a general way, the choosings of different men are to a great extent the same. The race as a whole largely agrees as to what it shall notice and name; and among the noticed parts we select in much the same way for accentuation and preference, or subordination and dislike. There is, however, one entirely extraordinary case in which no two men ever are known to choose alike. One great splitting of the whole universe into two halves is made by each of us; and for each of us almost all of the interest attaches to one of the halves; but we all draw the line of division between them in a different place. When I say that we all call the two halves by the same names, and that those names are '*me*' and '*not-me*' respectively, it will at once be seen what I mean. The altogether unique kind of interest which each human mind feels in those parts of creation which it can call *me* or *mine* may be a moral riddle, but it is a fundamental psychological fact. No mind can take the same interest in his neighbour's *me* as in his own. The neighbour's me falls together with all the rest of things in one foreign mass against which his own *me* stands out in startling relief. . . . He is for me a mere part of the world; for him it is I who am the mere part. Each of us dichotomizes the Kosmos in a different place.

Descending now to finer work than this first general sketch, let us in the next chapter try to trace the psychology of this fact of self-consciousness to which we have thus once more been led.

THE SELF

'THE Self' is a highly ambiguous term, and philosophers and psychologists have employed it in a confusing variety of ways. In this chapter James performed a useful service in preliminary classification. It is a chapter to which we may still turn to study in their early youth some of the Egos and Super-Egos, the Ego-Ideals, the 'Personas' and Personalities which are now to be seen in relative maturity in the theories of Freud, Jung and others.

The Me and the I. Whatever I may be thinking of, I am always at the same time more or less aware of *myself*, of my *personal existence*. At the same time it is *I* who am aware; so that the total self of me, being as it were duplex, partly known and partly knower, partly object and partly subject, must have two aspects discriminated in it, of which for shortness we may call one the *Me* and the other the *I*. . . .

I shall therefore treat successively of (A) the self as known, or the *me*, the 'empirical ego' as it is sometimes called; and of (B) the self as knower, or the I, the 'pure ego' of certain authors.

(A) THE SELF AS KNOWN

(a) *The constituents of the Me* may be divided into three classes, those which make up respectively –

The material me;
The social me; and
The spiritual me.

The Material Me. The *body* is the innermost part of the material me in each of us; and certain parts of the body seem more intimately ours than the rest. The clothes come next. The old saying that the human person is composed of three parts — soul, body and clothes — is more than a joke. ... Next, our immediate family is a part of ourselves. ... Our home comes next. ... An equally instinctive impulse drives us to collect property; and the collections thus made become, with different degrees of intimacy, parts of our empirical selves. ...

The Social Me. A man's social me is the recognition which he gets from his mates. ... Properly speaking, *a man has as many social selves as there are individuals who recognize him* and carry an image of him in their mind. To wound any one of these his images is to wound him. But as the individuals who carry the images fall naturally into classes, we may practically say that he has as many different social selves as there are distinct *groups* of persons about whose opinion he cares. He generally shows a different side of himself to each of these different groups. ... We do not show ourselves to our children as to our club-companions. to our customers as to the labourers we employ, to our own masters and employers as to our intimate friends. From this there results what practically is a division of the man into several selves; and this may be a discordant splitting, as where one is afraid to let one set of his acquaintances know him as he is elsewhere; or it may be a perfectly harmonious division of labour, as where one tender to his children is stern to the soldiers or prisoners under his command. ...

The Spiritual Me. By the 'spiritual me', so far as it belongs to the empirical self, I mean no one of my passing states of consciousness. I mean rather the entire collection of my states of consciousness, my psychic faculties and dispositions taken concretely. This collection can at any moment become an object to my thought at that moment and awaken emotions like those awakened by any of the other portions of the Me. . . .

Rivalry and Conflict of the Different Mes. With most objects of desire, physical nature restricts our choice to but one of many represented goods, and even so it is here. I am often confronted by the necessity of standing by one of my empirical selves and relinquishing the rest. Not that I would not, if I could, be both handsome and fat and well dressed, and a great athlete, and make a million a year, be a wit, a *bon-vivant*, and a lady-killer, as well as a philosopher; a philanthropist, statesman, warrior, and African explorer, as well as a 'tone-poet' and saint. But the thing is simply impossible. The millionaire's work would run counter to the saint's; the *bon-vivant* and the philanthropist would trip each other up; the philosopher and the lady-killer could not well keep house in the same tenement of clay. Such different characters may conceivably at the outset of life be alike *possible* to a man. But to make any one of them actual, the rest must more or less be suppressed. So the seeker of his truest, strongest, deepest self must review the list carefully, and pick out the one on which to stake his salvation. All other selves thereupon become unreal, but the fortunes of this self are real. Its failures are real failures, its triumphs real triumphs, carrying shame and gladness with them. This is as strong an example as there is of that selective industry of the mind on which I insisted some pages back (pp. 99–100). Our thought, incessantly deciding among many things of a kind, which ones for it shall be realities, here chooses one of many possible selves or characters, and forthwith reckons it no shame to fail in any of those not adopted expressly as its own.

So we have the paradox of a man shamed to death because he is only the second pugilist or the second oarsman in the world. That he is able to beat the whole population of the globe minus one is nothing; he has 'pitted' himself to beat that one; and as long as he doesn't do that nothing else counts. He is to his own regard as if he were not, indeed he *is* not. Yonder puny fellow, however, whom every one can beat, suffers no chagrin about it, for he has long ago abandoned the attempt to 'carry that line', as the merchants say, of self at all. With no attempt there can be no failure; with no failure, no humiliation. So our self-feeling in this world depends entirely on what we *back* ourselves to be and do. It is determined by the ratio of our actualities to our supposed potentialities; a fraction of which our pretensions are the denominator and the numerator our success: thus,

$$\text{Self-esteem} = \frac{\text{Success}}{\text{Pretensions}}.$$

Such a fraction may be increased as well by diminishing the denominator as by increasing the numerator. To give up pretensions is as blessed a relief as to get them gratified; and where disappointment is incessant and the struggle unending, this is what men will always do. . . . There is the strangest lightness about the heart when one's nothingness in a particular line is once accepted in good faith. *All* is not bitterness in the lot of the lover sent away by the final inexorable 'No'. Many Bostonians, *crede experto* (and inhabitants of other cities, too, I fear), would be happier women and men to-day, if they could once for all abandon the notion of keeping up a Musical Self, and without shame let people hear them call a symphony a nuisance. How pleasant is the day when we give up striving to be young, – or slender! Thank God! we say, *those* illusions are gone. Everything added to the Self is a burden as well as a pride. A certain man who lost every penny during our civil war went and actually rolled in the dust, saying he had not felt so free and happy since he was born. . . .

The Hierarchy of the Mes. A tolerably unanimous opinion ranges the different selves . . . in an *hierarchical scale, with the bodily me at the bottom, the spiritual me at top, and the* [*wider*] *material selves and the various social selves between.* . . .

A certain amount of bodily selfishness is required as a basis for all the other selves. But too much sensuality is despised, or at best condoned on account of the other qualities of the individual. The wider material selves are regarded as higher than the immediate body. He is esteemed a poor creature who is unable to forego a little meat and drink and warmth and sleep for the sake of getting on in the world. The social self as a whole, again, ranks higher than the material self as a whole. We must care more for our honour, our friends, our human ties, than for a sound skin or wealth. And the spiritual self is so supremely precious that, rather than lose it, a man ought to be willing to give up friends and good fame, and property, and life itself.

In each kind of Me, material, social, and spiritual, men distinguish between the immediate and actual, and the remote and potential, between the narrower and the wider view, to the detriment of the former and the advantage of the latter. One must forego a present bodily enjoyment for the sake of one's general health; one must abandon the dollar in the hand for the sake of the hundred dollars to come; one must make an enemy of his present interlocutor if thereby one makes friends of a more valued circle; one must go without learning and grace and wit, the better to compass one's soul's salvation.

Of all these wider, more potential selves, *the potential social Me* is the most interesting, by reason of certain apparent paradoxes to which it leads in conduct, and by reason of its connection with our moral and religious life. When for motives of honour and conscience I brave the condemnation of my own family, club, and 'set'; when, as a Protestant, I turn Catholic; as a Catholic, freethinker; as a 'regular practitioner', homœopath, or what not, I am always inwardly strengthened in my course and steeled against the loss of my actual social self by the thought of other and better *possible* social judges than those whose verdict goes against me now. The ideal social self which I thus seek in appealing to their decision may be very remote: it may be represented as barely possible. I may not hope for its realization during my lifetime; I may even expect the future generations, which would approve me if they knew me, to know nothing about me when I am dead and gone. Yet still the emotion that beckons me on is indubitably the pursuit of an ideal social self, of a self that is at least *worthy* of approving recognition by the highest *possible* judging companion, if such companion there be. This self is the true, the intimate, the ultimate, the permanent me which I seek. This judge is God, the Absolute mind, the 'Great Companion'. . . .

All progress in the social Self is the substitution of higher tribunals for lower; this ideal tribunal is the highest; and most men, either continually or occasionally, carry a reference to it in their breast. The humblest outcast on this earth can feel himself to be real and valid by means of this higher recognition. And, on the other hand, for most of us, a world with no such inner refuge when the outer social self failed and dropped from us would be the abyss of horror. I say 'for most of us', because it is probable that individuals differ a good deal in the degree in which they are haunted by this sense of an ideal spectator. It is a much more essential part of the consciousness of some men than of others. . . . But I am sure that even those who say they are altogether without it deceive themselves, and really have it in some degree. . . . Probably no one can make sacrifices for 'right', without to some degree personifying the principle of right for which the sacrifice is made, and expecting thanks from it. *Complete* social unselfishness, in other words, can hardly exist; *complete* social suicide hardly occur to a man's mind. Even such texts as Job's, 'Though He slay me, yet will I trust Him,' or Marcus Aurelius's, 'If gods hate me and my children, there is a reason for it,' can least of all be cited to prove the contrary. For beyond all doubt Job revelled in the thought of Jehovah's recognition of the worship after the slaying should have been done; and the Roman emperor felt sure the Absolute Reason would not be all indifferent to his acquiescence in the gods' dislike. . . .

(B) THE SELF AS KNOWER

The I, or 'pure ego', is a very much more difficult subject of inquiry than the Me. It is that which at any given moment *is* conscious, whereas the Me is only one of the things which it is conscious *of*. In other words, it is the *Thinker;* and the question immediately comes up *what* is the thinker? Is it the passing state of consciousness itself, or is it something deeper and less mutable? The passing state we have seen to be the very embodiment of change. Yet each of us spontaneously considers that by 'I', he means something always the same. This has led most philosophers to postulate behind the passing state of consciousness a permanent Substance or Agent whose modification or act it is. This Agent is the thinker; the 'state' is only its instrument or means. 'Soul', 'transcendental Ego',

'Spirit', are so many names for this more permanent sort of Thinker.

James's discussion of the hypothesis of the transcendental Ego is a piece of close-knit reasoning which cannot be adequately represented by extracts. Even the discussion in the *Briefer Course* is too condensed to be wholly satisfying, and the reader who is interested in this basic problem of philosophical psychology should consult the relevant chapters in the *Principles* (Chapter VI 'The Mind-Stuff Theory', and Chapter X 'The Consciousness of Self'). Here it is only possible to give James's conclusions, which are that 'The states of consciousness are all that psychology needs to do her work with. Metaphysics or theology may prove the Soul to exist; but for psychology the hypothesis of such a substantial principle of unity is superfluous' (PBC, p. 203). In the *Principles* he adds that 'The Soul is an outbirth of that sort of philosophizing whose great maxim, according to Dr Hodgson, is: "Whatever you are *totally* ignorant of, assert to be the explanation of everything else" ' (I. p. 347).

The chapter ends with a description of certain abnormal phenomena, such as dissociation and alternating personality, which are relevant to the problem of the Self. Mediumistic possession is the last of these phenomena to be considered.

In *'mediumships'* or *'possessions'* . . . the duration of the secondary state is usually short . . .

. . . The subject during the secondary consciousness speaks, writes, or acts as if animated by a foreign person, and often names this foreign person and gives his history. In old times the foreign 'control' was usually a demon, and is so now in communities which favour that belief. With us he gives himself out at the worst for an Indian or other grotesquely speaking but harmless personage. Usually he purports to be the spirit of a dead person known or unknown to those present, and the subject is then what we call a 'medium'. Mediumistic possession in all its grades seems to form a perfectly natural special type of alternate personality, and the susceptibility to it in some form is by no means an uncommon gift, in persons who have no other obvious nervous anomaly. The phenomena are very intricate, and are only just beginning to be studied in a proper scientific way. The lowest phase of mediumship is automatic writing, and the lowest grade of that is where the Subject knows what words are coming, but feels impelled to write them as if from without. Then comes writing unconsciously, even whilst engaged in reading or talk. Inspirational speaking, playing on musical instruments, etc., also belong to the relatively lower phases of possession, in which the normal self is not excluded from conscious participation in the performance, though their initiative seems to come from elsewhere. In the highest phase the trance is complete, the voice, language, and everything are changed, and there is no after-memory whatever until the next trance comes. One curious thing about trance-utterances is their generic similarity in different individuals. The 'control' here in America is either a grotesque, slangy, and flippant personage ('Indian' controls, calling the ladies 'squaws', the men 'braves', the house a 'wigwam', etc., etc., are excessively common); or, if he ventures on higher intellectual flights, he abounds in a curiously vague optimistic philosophy-and-water, in which phrases about spirit, harmony, beauty, law, progression, development, etc., keep recurring. It seems exactly as if one author composed more than half of the trance-messages, no matter by whom they are uttered. Whether all sub-conscious selves are peculiarly susceptible to a certain stratum of the *Zeitgeist*, and get their inspiration from it, I know not; but this is obviously the case with the secondary selves which become 'developed' in spiritualist circles. . . .

I have no theory to publish of these cases, the actual beginnings of several of which I have personally seen. I am, however, persuaded by abundant acquaintance with the trances of one medium that the 'control' may be altogether different from any *possible* waking self of the person. In the case I have in mind, it professes to be a certain departed French doctor; and is, I am convinced, acquainted with facts about the circumstances, and the living and dead relatives and acquaintances, of numberless sitters whom the medium never met before, and of whom she has never heard the names. I record my bare opinion here, unsupported by the evidence, not, of course, in order to convert anyone to my view, but because I am persuaded that a serious study of these trance-phenomena is one of the greatest needs of psychology, and think that my personal confession may possibly draw a reader or two into a field which the *soi-disant* scientist usually refuses to explore. . . .

James, to the scandal of some of his professional colleagues, took a strong interest in mediumistic possession and similar phenomena. He was for many years an active member of the Society for Psychical Research, and was its President from 1894 to 1896. As the above passage suggests, his attitude, though open-minded, was by no means uncritical; but he was impatient of the conventional 'scientific' attitude of pre-judging the issue and refusing to examine the evidence. Those who were not convinced by the volumes of S.P.R. *Proceedings* that there was at least a case for investigation would, he said, 'remain in their dogmatic slumbers though one rose from the dead'. James's impressions and (somewhat non-committal) conclusions, after twenty-five years' contact with psychical research, are given in 'Final Impressions of a Psychical Researcher'.[5]

ATTENTION

The Varieties of Attention. [Attention may be divided into (A) sensorial, where the object is directly perceived, and (B) intellectual, where the object is something remembered, imagined or thought of. Both these types of attention may be either (*a*) immediate, where the topic or stimulus is interesting in itself, or (*b*) derived, where the topic or stimulus derives its interest from its association with some other immediately interesting thing. Both (A) and (B), again, may be either (α) effortless and involuntary, or (β) active and voluntary. Voluntary attention is always derived, but the converse does not hold.]

In *involuntary attention* of the *immediate sensorial* sort the stimulus is either a sense-impression, very intense, voluminous or sudden; or it is an *instinctive* stimulus, a perception which, by reason of its nature rather than its mere force, appeals to some one of our congenital impulses and has a directly exciting quality. . . .

Sensitiveness to immediately exciting sensorial stimuli characterizes the attention of childhood and youth. In mature age we have generally selected those stimuli which are connected with one or more so-called permanent interests, and our attention has grown irresponsive to the rest. But childhood is characterized by great active energy, and has few organized interests by which to meet new impressions and decide whether they are worthy of notice or not, and the consequence is that extreme mobility of the attention with which we are all familiar in children, and which makes of their first lessons such chaotic affairs. . . .

The passive sensorial attention is *derived* when the impression, without being either strong or of an instinctively exciting nature, is connected by previous experience and education with things that are so. These things may be called the *motives* of the attention. The impression draws an interest from them, or perhaps it even fuses into a single complex object with them; the result is that it is brought into the focus of the mind. A faint tap *per se* is not an interesting sound; it may well escape being discriminated from the general rumour of the world. But when it is a signal, as that of a lover on the window-pane, hardly will it go unperceived. . . .

Involuntary intellectual attention is immediate when we follow in thought a train of images exciting or interesting *per se*; derived, when the images are interesting only as means to a remote end, or merely because they are associated with something that makes them dear. The brain-currents may then form so solidly unified a system, and the absorption in their object be so deep, as to banish not only ordinary sensations, but even the severest pain. . . . Dr Carpenter says of himself that 'he has frequently begun a lecture whilst suffering neuralgic pain so severe as to make him apprehend that he would find it impossible to proceed; yet no sooner has he by a determined effort fairly launched himself into the stream of thought, than he has found himself continuously borne along without the least distraction, until the end has come, and the attention has been released; when the pain has recurred with a force that has overmastered all resistance.' . . .

Voluntary Attention. Dr Carpenter speaks of launching himself by a determined *effort*. This effort characterizes what we called *active or voluntary attention*. It is a feeling which everyone knows, but which most people would call quite indescribable. We get it in the sensorial sphere whenever we seek to catch an impression of extreme *faintness*, be it of sight, hearing, taste, smell, or touch; we get it whenever we seek to *discriminate* a sensation merged in a mass of others that are similar; we get it whenever we *resist the attractions* of more potent stimuli and keep our mind occupied with some object that is naturally unimpressive. We get it in the intellectual sphere under exactly similar conditions: as when we strive to sharpen and make distinct an idea which we but vaguely seem to have; or painfully discriminate a shade of meaning from its similars; or resolutely hold fast to a thought so discordant with our impulses that, if left unaided, it would quickly yield place to images of an exciting and impassioned kind. All forms of attentive effort would be exercised at once by one whom we might suppose at a dinner-party resolutely to listen to a neighbour giving him insipid and unwelcome advice in a low voice, whilst all around the guests were loudly laughing and talking about exciting and interesting things.

There is no such thing as voluntary attention sustained for more than a few seconds at a time. What is called sustained voluntary attention is a repetition of successive efforts which bring back the topic to the mind. The topic once brought back, if a congenial one, *develops*; and if its development is interesting it engages the attention passively for a time. Dr Carpenter, a moment back, described the stream of thought, once entered, as 'bearing him along'. . .

Now there are always some objects that for the time being *will not develop.* They simply *go out;* and to keep the mind upon anything related to them requires such incessantly renewed effort that the most resolute Will ere long gives out and lets its thought follow the more stimulating solicitations after it has withstood them for what length of time it can. There are topics known to every man from which he shies like a frightened horse, and which to get a glimpse of is to shun. Such are his ebbing assets to the spendthrift in full career. But why single out the spendthrift, when to every man actuated by passion the thought of interests which negate the passion can hardly for more than a fleeting instant stay before the mind? It is like 'memento mori' in the heyday of the pride of life. Nature rises at such suggestions, and excludes them from the view: — How long, O healthy reader, can you now continue thinking of your tomb? — In milder instances the difficulty is as great, especially when the brain is fagged. One snatches at any and every passing pretext, no matter how trivial or external, to escape from the odiousness of the matter in hand. I know a person, for example, who will poke the fire, set chairs straight, pick dust-specks from the floor, arrange his table, snatch up the newspaper, take down any book which catches his eye, trim his nails, waste the morning *anyhow,* in short, and all without premeditation, — simply because the only thing he *ought* to attend to is the preparation of a noonday lesson in formal logic which he detests. Anything but *that!* . . .

No one can possibly attend continuously to an object that does not change. . . . Helmholtz, who has put his sensorial attention to the severest tests, makes some interesting remarks on this point. [He says] 'The natural tendency of attention when left to itself is to wander to ever new things; and so soon as the interest of its object is over, so soon as nothing new is to be noticed there, it passes, in spite of our will, to something else. *If we wish to keep it upon one and the same object, we must seek constantly to find out something new about the latter*, especially if other powerful impressions are attracting us away.'

These words of Helmholtz are of fundamental importance. And if true of sensorial attention, how much more true are they of the intellectual variety! The *conditio sine quâ non* of sustained attention to a given topic of thought is that we should roll it over and over incessantly and consider different aspects and relations of it in turn. Only in pathological states will a fixed and ever monotonously recurring idea possess the mind.

Genius and Attention. And now we can see why it is that what is called sustained attention is the easier, the richer in acquisitions and the fresher and more original the mind. In such minds, subjects bud and sprout and grow. At every moment, they please by a new consequence and rivet the attention afresh. But an intellect unfurnished with materials, stagnant, unoriginal, will hardly be likely to consider any subject long. A glance exhausts its possibilities of interest. Geniuses are commonly believed to excel other men in their power of sustained attention. In most of them, it is to be feared, the so-called 'power' is of the passive sort. Their ideas coruscate, every subject branches infinitely before their fertile minds, and so for hours they may be rapt. *But it is their genius making them attentive, not their attention making geniuses of them.* And, when we come down to the root of the matter, we see that they differ from ordinary men less in the character of their attention than in the nature of the objects upon which it is successively bestowed. In the genius, these form a concatenated series, suggesting each other mutually by some rational law. Therefore we call the attention 'sustained' and the topic of meditation for hours 'the same'. In the common man the series is for the most part incoherent, the objects have no rational bond, and we call the attention wandering and unfixed.

It is probable that genius tends actually to prevent a man from acquiring habits of voluntary attention, and that moderate intellectual endowments are the soil in which we may best expect, here as elsewhere, the virtues of the will, strictly so called, to thrive. But, whether the attention come by grace of genius or by dint of will, the longer one does attend to a topic the more mastery of it one has. And the faculty of voluntarily bringing back a wandering attention over and over again is the very root of judgment, character, and will. No one is *compos sui* if he have it not. An education which should improve this faculty would be *the* education *par excellence*. But it is easier to define this ideal than to give practical directions for bringing it about. The only general pedagogic maxim bearing on attention is that the more interests the child has in advance in the subject, the better he will attend. Induct him therefore in such a way as to knit each new thing on to some acquisition already there; and if possible awaken curiosity, so that the new thing shall seem to come as an answer, or part of an answer, to a question pre-existing in his mind. . . .

This vitally important 'pedagogic maxim' is discussed more fully in *Talks to Teachers*. Cf. p. 235 ff.

ASSOCIATION

THE manner in which trains of imagery and consideration follow each other through our thinking, the restless flight of one idea before the next, the transitions our minds make between things wide as the poles asunder, transitions which at first sight startle us by their abruptness, but which, when scrutinized closely, often reveal intermediating links of perfect naturalness and propriety – all this magical, imponderable streaming has from time immemorial excited the admiration of all whose attention happened to be caught by its omnipresent mystery. And it has furthermore challenged the race of philosophers to banish something of the mystery by formulating the process in simpler terms. The problem which the philosophers have set themselves is that of ascertaining, between the thoughts which thus appear to sprout one out of the other, *principles of connection* whereby their peculiar succession or coexistence may be explained. . . . How does a man come, after having the thought of A, to have the thought of B the next moment? or how does he come to think A and B always together? These were the phenomena which Hartley undertook to explain by cerebral physiology. I believe that he was, in essential respects, on the right track, and I propose simply to revise his conclusions by the aid of distinctions which he did not make.

Objects are associated, not ideas. We shall avoid confusion if we consistently speak as if *association,* so far as the word stands for an *effect, were between* THINGS THOUGHT OF – *as if it were* THINGS, *not ideas, which are associated in the mind.* We shall talk of the association of *objects,* not of the association of *ideas.* And so far as association stands for a *cause,* it is between *processes in the brain* – it is these which, by being associated in certain ways, determine what successive objects shall be thought.

The Elementary Principle. I shall now try to show that there is no other *elementary* causal law of association than the law of neural habit. All the *materials* of our thought are due to the way in which one elementary process of the cerebral hemispheres tends to excite whatever other elementary process it may have excited at any former time. . . .

Let us then assume as the basis of all our subsequent reasoning this law: *When two elementary brain-processes have been active together or in immediate succession, one of them, on re-occurring, tends to propagate its excitement into the other.*

But, as a matter of fact, every elementary process has unavoidably found itself at different times excited in conjunction with *many* other processes. Which of these others it shall awaken now becomes a problem. Shall *b* or *c* be aroused next by the present *a*? . . . The process *b*, rather than *c*, will awake, if in addition to the vibrating tract *a* some other tract *d* is in a state of sub-excitement, and formerly was excited with *b* alone and not with *a*. In short, we may say:

The amount of activity at any given point in the brain-cortex is the sum of the tendencies of all other points to discharge into it, such tendencies being proportionate (1) *to the number of times the excitement of each other point may have accompanied that of the point in question;* (2) *to the intensity of such excitements; and* (3) *to the absence of any rival point functionally disconnected with the first point, into which the discharges might be diverted.*

Expressing the fundamental law in this most complicated way leads to the greatest ultimate simplification. Let us, for the present, only treat of spontaneous trains of thought and ideation, such as occur in revery or musing. The case of voluntary thinking toward a certain end shall come up later.

Spontaneous Trains of Thought. Take, to fix our ideas, the two verses from 'Locksley Hall':

I, the heir of all *the ages* in the foremost files of time,

and —

For I doubt not through *the ages* one increasing purpose runs.

Why is it that when we recite from memory one of these lines, and get as far as *the ages*, that portion of the *other* line which follows and, so to speak, sprouts out of *the ages* does not also sprout out of our memory and confuse the sense of our words? Simply because the word that follows *the ages* has its brain-process awakened not simply by the brain-process of *the ages* alone, but by it *plus* the brain processes of all the words preceding *the ages*. The word *ages* at its moment of strongest activity would, *per se*, indifferently discharge into either 'in' or 'one'. So would the previous words (whose tension is momentarily much less strong than that of *ages*) each of them indifferently discharge into either of a large number of other words with which they have been at different times combined. But when the processes of '*I, the heir of all the ages*,' simultaneously vibrate in the brain, the last one of them in a maximal, the others in a fading, phase of excitement, then the strongest line of discharge will be that which they *all alike* tend to take. '*In*' and not '*one*' or any other word will be the next to awaken, for its brain-process has pre-viously vibrated in unison not only with that of *ages*, but with that of all those other words whose activity is dying away. It is a good case of the effectiveness over thought of what we called on p. 98 a 'fringe'.

But if some one of these preceding words — 'heir', for example — had an intensely strong association with some brain-tracts entirely disjoined in experience from the poem of 'Locksley Hall' — if the reciter, for instance, were tremulously awaiting the opening of a will which might make him a millionaire – it is probable that the path of discharge through the words of the poem would be suddenly interrupted at the word 'heir'. His *emotional interest in that word* would be such that its *own special associations would prevail* over the combined ones of the other words. He would, as we say, be abruptly reminded of his personal situation, and the poem would lapse altogether from his thoughts.

The writer of these pages has every year to learn the names of a large number of students who sit in alphabetical order in a lecture-room. He finally learns to call them by name, as they sit in their accustomed places. On meeting one in the street, however, early in the year, the face hardly ever recalls the name, but it may recall the place of its owner in the lecture-room, his neighbour's faces, and consequently his general alphabetical position: and then, usually as the common associate of all these combined data, the student's name surges up in his mind.

A father wishes to show to some guests the progress of his rather dull child in kindergarten-instruction. Holding the knife upright on the table, he says, 'What do you call that, my boy?' 'I calls it a *knife*, I does,' is the sturdy reply, from which the child cannot be induced to swerve by any alteration in the form of question, until the father, recollecting that in the kindergarten a pencil was used and not a knife, draws a long one from his pocket, holds it in the same way, and then gets the wished-for answer, 'I calls it *vertical*'. All the concomitants of the kindergarten experience had to recombine their effect before the word 'vertical' could be reawakened.

Total Recall. The ideal working of the law of compound association, as Professor Bain calls it, were it unmodified by any extraneous influence, would be such as to keep the mind in a perpetual treadmill of concrete reminiscences from which no detail could be omitted. . . . From this complete redintegration there could be no escape save through the irruption of some new and strong present impression of the senses, or through the excessive tendency of some one of the elementary brain-tracts to discharge independently into an aberrant quarter of the brain. Such was the tendency of the word 'heir' in the verse from 'Locksley Hall', which was our first example. How such tendencies are constituted we shall have soon to inquire with some care. Unless they are present, the panorama of the past, once opened, must unroll itself with fatal literality to the end, unless some outward sound, sight, or touch divert the current of thought.

Let us call this process *impartial redintegration,* or, still better, *total recall.* Whether it ever occurs in an absolutely complete form is doubtful. We all immediately recognize, however, that in some minds there is a much greater tendency than in others for the flow of thought to take this form. Those insufferably garrulous old women, those dry and fanciless beings who spare you no detail, however petty, of the facts they are recounting, and upon the thread of whose narrative all the irrelevant items cluster as pertinaciously as the essential ones, the slaves of literal fact, the stumblers over the smallest abrupt step in thought, are figures known to all of us. . . .

Partial Recall. [The reason why] the ordinary spontaneous flow of our ideas does not follow the law of total recall [is that] *in no revival of a past experience are all the items of our thought equally operative in determining what the next thought shall be. Always some ingredient is prepotent over the rest.* . . . Just as in the original sensible experience our attention focalized itself upon a few of the impressions of the scene before us, so here in the reproduction of those impressions an equal partiality is shown, and some items are emphasized above the rest. . . . In subjective terms we say that *the prepotent items are those which appeal most to our* INTEREST. . . .

Only where the interest is diffused equally over all the parts is this law departed from. It will be least obeyed by those minds which have the smallest variety and intensity of interests – those who, by the general flatness and poverty of their æsthetic nature, are kept for ever rotating among the literal sequences of their local and personal history.

Most of us, however, are better organized than this, and our musings pursue an erratic course, swerving continually into some new direction traced by the shifting play of interest as it ever falls on some partial item in each complex representation that is evoked. Thus it so often comes about that we find ourselves thinking at two nearly adjacent moments of things separated by the whole diameter of space and time. Not till we carefully recall each step of our cogitation do we see how naturally we came to pass from one to the other. Thus, for instance, after looking at my clock just now (1879), I found myself thinking of a recent resolution in the Senate about our legal-tender notes. The clock called up the image of the man who had repaired its gong. He suggested the jeweller's shop where I had last seen him; that shop, some shirt-studs which I had bought there; they, the value of gold and its recent decline; the latter, the equal value of greenbacks, and this, naturally, the question of how long they were to last, and of the Bayard proposition. Each of these images offered various points of interest. Those which formed the turning-points of my thought are easily assigned. The gong was momentarily the most interesting part of the clock, because, from having begun with a beautiful tone, it had become discordant and aroused disappointment. But for this the clock might have suggested the friend who gave it to me, or any one of a thousand circumstances connected with clocks. The jeweller's shop suggested the studs, because they alone of all its contents were tinged with the egoistic interest of possession. This interest in the studs, their value, made me single out the material as its chief source, etc., to the end. Every reader who will arrest himself at any moment and say, 'How came I to be thinking of just this?' will be sure to trace a train of representations linked together by lines of contiguity and points of interest inextricably combined. This is the ordinary process of the association of ideas as it spontaneously goes on in average minds. *We may call it ordinary, or mixed, association,* or, if we like better, *partial recall.*

Which Associates come up, in Partial Recall? Can we determine, now, when a certain portion of the going thought has, by dint of its interest, become so prepotent as to make its own exclusive associates the dominant features of the coming thought – can we, I say, determine *which* of its own associates shall be evoked? For they are many. [Hodgson's suggestion is that each thought evokes those of its associates that have been most habitually combined with it before. But] in restricting the discharge from the interesting item into that channel which is simply most *habitual* in the sense of most frequent, Hodgson's account is assuredly imperfect. An image by no means always revives its most frequent associate, although frequency is certainly one of the most potent determinants of revival. If I abruptly utter the word *swallow*, the reader, if by habit an ornithologist, will think of a bird; if a physiologist or a medical specialist in throat-diseases, he will think of deglutition. If I say *date*, he will, if a fruit-merchant or an Arabian traveller, think of the produce of the palm; if an habitual student of history, figures with A.D. or B.C. before them will rise in his mind. . . . But frequent lines of transition are often set at naught. The sight of a certain book has most frequently awakened in me thoughts of the opinions therein propounded. The idea of suicide has never been connected with the volume. But a moment since, as my eye fell upon it, suicide was the thought that flashed into my mind. Why? Because but yesterday I received a letter informing me that the author's recent death was an act of self-destruction. Thoughts tend, then, to awaken their most recent as well as their most habitual associates. This is a matter of notorious experience, too notorious, in fact, to need illustration. . . . If Shakespeare's plays are mentioned, and we were last night reading *Richard II*, vestiges of that play rather than of *Hamlet* or *Othello* float through our mind. . . .

Vividness in an original experience may also have the same effect as habit or recency in bringing about likelihood of revival. If we have once witnessed an execution, any subsequent conversation or reading about capital punishment will almost certainly suggest images of that particular scene. Thus it is that events lived through only once, and in youth, may come in after-years, by reason of their exciting quality or emotional intensity, to serve as types or instances used by our mind to illustrate any and every occurring topic whose interest is most remotely pertinent to theirs. . . .

A fourth factor in tracing the course of reproduction is *congruity in emotional tone* between the reproduced idea and our mood. The same objects do not recall the same associates when we are cheerful as when we are melancholy. Nothing, in fact, is more striking than our inability to keep up trains of joyous imagery when we are depressed in spirits. Storm, darkness, war, images of disease, poverty, perishing, and dread afflict unremittingly the imaginations of melancholiacs. And those of sanguine temperament, when their spirits are high, find it impossible to give any permanence to evil forebodings or to gloomy thoughts. . . .

Habit, recency, vividness, and emotional congruity are, then, all reasons why one representation rather than another should be awakened by the interesting portion of a departing thought. We may say with truth that *in the majority of cases the coming representation will have been either habitual, recent, or vivid, and will be congruous.* If all these qualities unite in any one absent associate, we may predict almost infallibly that that associate of the going object will form an important ingredient in the object which comes next. In spite of the fact, however, that the succession of representations is thus redeemed from perfect indeterminism and limited to a few classes whose characteristic quality is fixed by the nature of our past experience, it must still be confessed that an immense number of terms in the linked chain of our representations fall outside of all assignable rule. To take the instance of the clock given on p. 122. Why did the jeweller's shop suggest the shirt-studs rather than a chain which I had bought there more recently, which had cost more, and whose sentimental associations were much more interesting? Any reader's experience will easily furnish similar instances. So we must admit that to a certain extent, even in those forms of ordinary mixed association which lie nearest to impartial redintegration, *which* associate of the interesting item shall emerge must be called largely a matter of accident – accident, that is, for our intelligence. No doubt it is determined by cerebral causes, but they are too subtle and shifting for our analysis. . . .

Voluntary Trains of Thought. Hitherto we have assumed the process of suggestion of one object by another to be spontaneous. The train of imagery wanders at its own sweet will, now trudging in sober grooves of habit, now with a hop, skip, and jump, darting across the whole field of time and space. This is revery, or musing; but great segments of the flux of our ideas consist of something very different from this. They are guided by a distinct purpose or conscious interest; and the course of our ideas is then called *voluntary*.

Physiologically considered, we must suppose that a purpose means the persistent activity of certain rather definite brain-processes throughout the whole course of thought. Our most usual cogitations are not pure reveries, absolute driftings, but revolve about some central interest or topic to which most of the images are relevant, and towards which we return promptly after occasional digressions. This interest is subserved by the persistently active brain-tracts we have supposed. In the mixed associations which we have hitherto studied, the parts of each object which form the pivots on which our thoughts successively turn have their interest largely determined by their connection with some *general interest* which for the time has seized upon the mind. If we call Z the brain-tract of general interest, then, if the object abc turns up, and b has more associations with Z than have either a or c, b will become the object's interesting, pivotal portion, and will call up its own associates exclusively. For the energy of b's brain-tract will be augmented by Z's activity, — an activity which, from lack of previous connection between Z and a and Z and c, does not influence a or c. If, for instance, I think of Paris whilst I am *hungry*, I shall not improbably find that its *restaurants* have become the pivot of my thought, etc., etc.

Problems. But in the theoretic as well as in the practical life there are interests of a more acute sort, taking the form of definite images of some achievement which we desire to effect. The train of ideas arising under the influence of such an interest constitutes usually the thought of the *means* by which the end shall be attained. If the end by its simple presence does not instantaneously suggest the means, the search for the latter becomes a *problem;* and the discovery of the means forms a new sort of end, of an entirely peculiar nature — an end, namely, which we intensely desire before we have attained it, but of the nature of which, even whilst most strongly craving it, we have no distinct imagination whatever.

The same thing occurs whenever we seek to recall something forgotten, or to state the reason for a judgment which we have made intuitively. The desire strains and presses in a direction which it feels to be right, but towards a point which it is unable to see. In short, the *absence of an item* is a determinant of our representations quite as positive as its presence can ever be. The gap becomes no mere void, but what is called an *aching* void. If we try to explain in terms of brain-action how a thought which only potentially exists can yet be effective, we seem driven to believe that the brain-tract thereof must actually be excited, but only in a minimal and sub-conscious way. Try, for instance, to symbolize what goes on in a man who is racking his brains to remember a thought which occurred to him last week. The associates of the thought are there, many of them at least, but they refuse to awaken the thought itself. We cannot suppose that they do not irradiate *at all* into its brain-tract, because his mind quivers on the very edge of its recovery. Its actual rhythm sounds in his ears; the words seem on the imminent point of following, but fail (see p. 96). Now the only difference between the effort to recall things forgotten and the search after the means to a given end is that the latter have not, whilst the former have, already formed a part of our experience. If we first study *the mode of recalling a thing forgotten*, we can take up with better understanding the voluntary quest of the unknown.

Their Solution. The forgotten thing is felt by us as a gap in the midst of certain other things. We possess a dim idea of where we were and what we were about when it last occurred to us. We recollect the general subject to which it pertains. But all these details refuse to shoot together into a solid whole, for the lack of the missing thing, so we keep running over them in our mind, dissatisfied, craving something more. From each detail there radiate lines of association forming so many tentative guesses. Many of these are immediately seen to be irrelevant, are therefore void of interest, and lapse immediately from consciousness. Others are associated with the other details present, and with the missing thought as well. When *these* surge up, we have a peculiar feeling that we are 'warm', as the children say when they play hide and seek; and such associates as these we clutch at and keep before the attention. Thus we recollect successively that when we last were considering the matter in question we were at the dinner-table; then that our friend J. D. was there; then that the subject talked about was so and so; finally, that the thought came *à propos* of a certain anecdote, and then that it had something to do with a French quotation. Now all these added associates *arise independently of the will*, by the spontaneous processes we know so well. *All that the will does is to emphasize and linger over those which seem pertinent, and ignore the rest.* Through this hovering of the attention in the neighbourhood of the desired object, the accumulation of associates becomes so great that the combined tensions of their neural processes break through the bar, and the nervous wave pours into the tract which has so long been awaiting its advent. And as the expectant, sub-conscious itching, so to speak, bursts into the fullness of vivid feeling, the mind finds an inexpressible relief.

The whole process can be rudely symbolized in a diagram. Call the forgotten thing Z, the first facts with which we felt it was related *a*, *b*, and *c*, and the details finally operative in calling it up *l*, *m*, and *n*. Each circle will then stand for the brain-process principally concerned in the thought of the fact lettered within it. The activity in Z will at first be a mere tension; but as the activities in *a*, *b*, and *c*

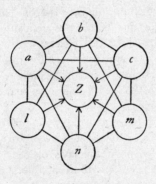

little by little irradiate into *l*, *m*, and *n*, and as *all* these processes are somehow connected with Z, their combined irradiations upon Z, represented by the centripetal arrows, succeed in rousing Z also to full activity.

Turn now to the case of finding the unknown means to a distinctly conceived end. The end here stands in the place of *a*, *b*, *c*, in the diagram. It is the starting-point of the irradiations of suggestion; and here, as in that case, what the voluntary attention does is only to dismiss some of the suggestions as irrelevant, and hold fast to others which are felt to be more pertinent — let these be symbolized by *l*, *m*, *n*. These latter at last accumulate sufficiently to discharge all together into Z, the excitement of which process is, in the mental sphere, equivalent to the solution of our problem. The only difference between this and the previous case is that in this one there need be no original sub-excitement in Z, co-operating from the very first. In the solving of a problem, all that we are aware of in advance seems to be its *relations*. It must be a cause, or it must be an effect, or it must contain an attribute, or it must be a means, or what not. We know, in short, a lot *about* it, whilst as yet we have no *acquaintance* with it. Our perception that one of the objects which turn up is, at last, our *quæsitum*, is due to our recognition that its relations are identical with those we had in mind, and this may be a rather slow act of judgment. Everyone knows that an object may be for some time present to his mind before its relations to other matters are perceived. Just so the relations may be there before the object is.

From the guessing of newspaper enigmas to the plotting of the policy of an empire there is no other process than this. We must trust to the laws of cerebral nature to present us spontaneously with the appropriate idea, but we must know it for the right one when it comes. . . .

This is a remarkable anticipation of Spearman's view[6] (which forms the basis of much modern intelligence testing) that intellectual activity essentially involves the discerning of relevant qualities and relations, and the eduction of correlates.

These terms can best be explained by example. Among the commonest types of problem employed in intelligence tests is the following —

Kitten is to cat as puppy is to?
Motive is to method as why is to?

6. Expounded in *Creative Mind* (1931) and elsewhere.

– the subject being required to supply the missing word, or to select it from a number of alternatives. To do this, he must first discern the relation between 'kitten' and 'cat' (or 'motive' and 'method'), and then educe a correlate – i.e. supply a fourth term which is related to the third term in the same way as the second is to the first. All 'insightful cognition', according to Spearman, involves one or both of these activities.

Eduction, the more creative of the two processes, is essential to the higher forms of constructive thought, such as invention or scientific discovery. (A case in point would be James Watt's invention of the steam-engine as a result of watching steam lifting the lid of a boiling kettle.) James is making precisely Spearman's point, though in different language, when he says that 'finding the unknown means to a distinctly conceived end' involves supplying a missing term, of which at first we know no more than its relations to other terms. The chapter on 'Reasoning' (pp. 138–50) contains many further anticipations of Spearman.

I trust that the student will now feel that the way to a deeper understanding of the order of our ideas lies in the direction of cerebral physiology. The *elementary* process of revival can be nothing but the law of habit. Truly the day is distant when physiologists shall actually trace from cell-group to cell-group the irradiations which we have hypothetically invoked. Probably it will never arrive. The schematism we have used is, moreover, taken immediately from the analysis of objects into their elementary parts, and only extended by analogy to the brain. And yet it is only as incorporated in the brain that such a schematism can repre-

sent anything *causal*. This is, to my mind, the conclusive
reason for saying that the order of *presentation of the mind's
materials* is due to cerebral physiology alone.

The law of accidental prepotency of certain processes
over others falls also within the sphere of cerebral proba-
bilities. Granting such instability as the brain-tissue requires, certain points must always discharge more quickly
and strongly than others; and this prepotency would shift
its place from moment to moment by accidental causes,
giving us a perfect mechanical diagram of the capricious
play of similar association in the most gifted mind. A study
of dreams confirms this view. The usual abundance of
paths of irradiation seems, in the dormant brain, reduced.
A few only are pervious, and the most fantastic sequences
occur because the currents run — 'like sparks in burnt-up
paper' — wherever the nutrition of the moment creates an
opening, but nowhere else.

The *effects of interested attention and volition* remain.
These activities seem to hold fast to certain elements and,
by emphasizing them and dwelling on them, to make their
associates the only ones which are evoked. *This* is the point
at which an anti-mechanical psychology must, if anywhere, make its stand in dealing with association. Everything else is pretty certainly due to cerebral laws. . . . But
even though there be a mental spontaneity, it can certainly
not create ideas or summon them *ex abrupto*. Its power is
limited to *selecting* amongst those which the associative
machinery introduces. If it can emphasize, reinforce, or
protract for half a second either one of these, it can do all
that the most eager advocate of free will need demand; for
it then decides the direction of the *next* associations by
making them hinge upon the emphasized term; and determining in this wise the course of the man's thinking, it
also determines his acts.

MEMORY

Retention and Recall. [The] exercise [of memory] pre-supposes two things:

(1) The *retention* of the remembered fact; and

(2) Its *reminiscence, recollection, reproduction,* or *recall.*

Now *the cause both of retention and of recollection is the law of habit in the nervous system, working as it does in the 'association of ideas'.*

[James then gives further examples of the activity of 'searching the mind' for a missing fact or name, and concludes:]

In short, we make search in our memory for a forgotten idea, just as we rummage our house for a lost object. In both cases we visit what seems to us the probable *neighbourhood* of that which we miss. We turn over the things under which, or within which, or alongside of which, it may possibly be; and if it lies near them, it soon comes to view. But these matters, in the case of a mental object sought, are nothing but its *associates.* The machinery of recall is thus the same as the machinery of association, and the machinery of association, as we know, is nothing but the elementary law of habit in the nerve-centres.

It also explains retention. And this same law of habit is the machinery of retention also. Retention means *liability* to recall, and it means nothing more than such liability. The only proof of there being retention is that recall actually takes place. The retention of an experience is, in short, but another name for the *possibility* of thinking it again, or the *tendency* to think it again, with its past sur-roundings. Whatever accidental cue may turn this tendency into an actuality, the permanent *ground* of the tendency itself lies in the organized neural paths by which the cue calls up the memorable experience . . .

The *retention* of [a fact or an experience], it will be observed, is no mysterious storing up of an 'idea' in an unconscious state. It is not a fact of the mental order at all. It is a purely physical phenomenon, a morphological feature, the presence of these 'paths', namely, in the finest recesses of the brain's tissue. The recall or recollection, on the other hand, is a *psycho-physical* phenomenon, with both a bodily and a mental side. The bodily side is the excitement of the paths in question; the mental side is the conscious representation of the past occurrence, and the belief that we experienced it before. . . .

The Conditions of Goodness in Memory. . . . *Memory being thus altogether conditioned on brain-paths, its excellence in a given individual will depend partly on the* NUMBER *and partly on the* PERSISTENCE *of these paths.*

The persistence or permanence of the paths is a physiological property of the brain-tissue of the individual, whilst their number is altogether due to the facts of his mental experience. Let the quality of permanence in the paths be called the native tenacity, or physiological retentiveness. This tenacity differs enormously from infancy to old age, and from one person to another. Some minds are like wax under a seal – no impression, however disconnected with others, is wiped out. Others, like a jelly, vibrate to every touch, but under usual conditions retain no permanent mark. These latter minds, before they can recollect a fact, must weave it into their permanent stores of knowledge. They have no *desultory* memory. Those persons, on the contrary, who retain names, dates and addresses, anecdotes, gossip, poetry, quotations, and all sorts of miscellaneous facts, without an effort, have desultory memory in a high degree, and certainly owe it to the unusual tenacity of their brain-substance for any path once formed therein. . . .

But there comes a time of life for all of us when we can do no more than hold our own in the way of acquisitions, when the old paths fade as fast as the new ones form in our brain, and when we forget in a week quite as much as we can learn in the same space of time. This equilibrium may last many, many years. In extreme old age it is upset in the reverse direction, and forgetting prevails over acquisition, or rather there is no acquisition. Brain-paths are so transient that in the course of a few minutes of conversation the same question is asked and its answer forgotten half a dozen times. Then the superior tenacity of the paths formed in childhood becomes manifest: the dotard will retrace the facts of his earlier years after he has lost all those of later date.

So much for the permanence of the paths. Now for their number. [If *n* stands for a past event, and *N* for the nerve-centres active in its recall, then it is obvious that the more paths there are in the brain leading to *N*,] the prompter and surer, on the whole, the memory of *n* will be, the more frequently one will be reminded of it, the more avenues of approach to it one will possess. In mental terms, *the more other facts a fact is associated with in the mind, the better possession of it our memory retains*. Each of its associates becomes a hook to which it hangs, a means to fish it up by when sunk beneath the surface. Together, they form a network of attachments by which it is woven into the entire tissue of our thought. The 'secret of a good memory' is thus the secret of forming diverse and multiple associations with every fact we care to retain. But this forming of associations with a fact, what is it but *thinking about* the fact as much as possible? Briefly, then, of two men with the same outward experiences and the same amount of mere native tenacity, *the one who* THINKS *over his experiences most, and weaves them into systematic relations with each other, will be the one with the best memory.* We see examples of this on every hand. Most men have a good memory for facts connected with their own pursuits. The college athlete who remains a dunce at his books will astonish you by his knowledge of men's 'records' in various feats and games, and will be a walking dictionary of sporting statistics. The reason is that he is constantly going over these things in his mind, and comparing and making series of them. They form for him not so many odd facts, but a concept-system – so they stick. So the merchant remembers prices, the politician other politicians' speeches and votes, with a copiousness which amazes outsiders, but which the amount of thinking they bestow on these subjects easily explains. The great memory for facts which a Darwin and a Spencer reveal in their books is not incompatible with the possession on their part of a brain with only a middling degree of physiological retentiveness. Let a man early in life set himself the task of verifying such a theory as that of evolution, and facts will soon cluster and cling to him like grapes to their stem. Their relations to the theory will hold them fast; and the more of these the mind is able to discern, the greater the erudition will become. Meanwhile the theorist may have little, if any, desultory memory. Unutil-izable facts may be unnoted by him and forgotten as soon as heard. An ignorance almost as encyclopædic as his erudition may co-exist with the latter, and hide, as it were, in the interstices of its web. Those who have had much to do with scholars and *savants* will readily think of examples of the class of mind I mean.

In a system, every fact is connected with every other by some thought-relation. The consequence is that every fact is retained by the combined suggestive power of all the other facts in the system, and forgetfulness is well-nigh impossible.

The reason why cramming is such a bad mode of study is now made clear. I mean by cramming that way of preparing for examinations by committing 'points' to memory during a few hours or days of intense application immediately preceding the final ordeal, little or no work having been performed during the previous course of the term. Things learned thus in a few hours, on one occasion, for one purpose, cannot possibly have formed many associations with other things in the mind. Their brain-processes are led into by few paths, and are relatively little liable to be awakened again. Speedy oblivion is the almost inevitable fate of all that is committed to memory in this simple way. Whereas, on the contrary, the same materials taken in gradually, day after day, recurring in different contexts, considered in various relations, associated with other external incidents, and repeatedly reflected on, grow into such a system, form such connections with the rest of the mind's fabric, lie open to so many paths of approach, that they remain permanent possessions. This is the *intellectual* reason why habits of continuous application should be enforced in educational establishments. Of course there is no moral turpitude in cramming. Did it lead to the desired end of secure learning, it were infinitely the best method of study. But it does not; and students themselves should understand the reason why.

One's native retentiveness is unchangeable. It will now appear clear that *all improvement of the memory lies in the line of* ELABORATING THE ASSOCIATES of each of the several things to be remembered. *No amount of culture would seem capable of modifying a man's* GENERAL *retentiveness.* This is a physiological quality, given once for all with his organization, and which he can never hope to change. It differs no doubt in disease and health; and it is a fact of observation that it is better in fresh and vigorous hours than when we are fagged or ill. We may say, then, that a man's native tenacity will fluctuate somewhat with his hygiene, and that whatever is good for his tone of health will also be good for his memory. We may even say that whatever amount of intellectual exercise is bracing to the general tone and nutrition of the brain will also be profitable to the general retentiveness. But more than this we cannot say; and this, it is obvious, is far less than most people believe. . . .

REASONING

What Reasoning is. We talk of man being the rational animal. . . . Nevertheless, it is by no means easy to decide just what is meant by reason, or how the peculiar thinking process called reasoning differs from other thought-sequences which may lead to similar results.

Much of our thinking consists of trains of images suggested one by another, of a sort of spontaneous revery. . . . The links between the terms are either 'contiguity' or 'similarity'. . . . As a rule, in this sort of irresponsible thinking, the terms which fall to be coupled together are empirical concretes, not abstractions. A sunset may call up the vessel's deck from which I saw one last summer, the companions of my voyage, my arrival into port, etc. . . .

The great difference between that simpler kind of rational thinking which consists in the concrete objects of past experience merely suggesting each other, and reasoning distinctively so called, is this: that whilst the empirical thinking is only reproductive, reasoning is productive. . . . Reasoning helps us out of unprecedented situations —

situations for which all our common associative wisdom . . . leaves us without resource.

Exact Definition of it. Let us make this ability to deal with *novel data the technical differentia of reasoning.* This will sufficiently mark it out from common associative thinking, and will immediately enable us to say just what peculiarity it contains.

It contains analysis and abstraction. Whereas the merely empirical thinker stares at a fact in its entirety, and remains helpless, or gets 'stuck', if it suggests no concomitant or similar, the reasoner breaks it up and notices some one of its separate attributes. This attribute he takes to be the essential part of the whole fact before him. This attribute has properties or consequences which the fact until then was not known to have, but which, now that it is noticed to contain the attribute, it must have.

Call the fact or concrete datum S;
> the essential attribute M;
> the attribute's property P.

Then the reasoned inference of P from S cannot be made without M's intermediation. . . .

What is meant by a Mode of Conceiving. The perception that S is M is a *mode of conceiving* S. When we conceive of S merely as M (of vermilion merely as a mercury-compound, for example), we neglect all the other attributes which it may have, and attend exclusively to this one. We mutilate the fulness of S's reality. Every reality has an infinity of aspects or properties. . . . Vermilion is not only a mercury-compound, it is vividly red, heavy, and expensive, it comes from China, and so on, *ad infinitum.* All objects are well-springs of properties, which are only little by little developed to our knowledge, and it is truly said that to know one thing thoroughly would be to know the whole universe. Mediately or immediately, that one thing is related to everything else; and to know *all* about it, all its relations need be known. But each relation forms one of its attributes, one angle by which someone may conceive it, and while so conceiving it may ignore the rest of it. . . .

All ways of conceiving a concrete fact, if they are true ways at all, are equally true ways. *There is no property* ABSOLUTELY *essential to any one thing.* The same property which figures as the essence of a thing on one occasion becomes a very inessential feature upon another. Now that I am writing, it is essential that I conceive my paper as a surface for inscription. If I failed to do that, I should have to stop my work. But if I wished to light a fire, and no other materials were by, the essential way of conceiving the paper would be as combustible material; and I need then have no thought of any of its other destinations. . . . *The only meaning of essence is teleological.* . . . The essence of a thing is that one of its properties which is so *important for my interests* that in comparison with it I may neglect the rest. . . .

Reasoning is always for a subjective interest. To revert now to our symbolic representation of the reasoning process:

$$M \text{ is } P$$
$$S \text{ is } M$$
$$\overline{S \text{ is } P}$$

M is discerned and picked out for the time being to be the essence of the concrete fact, phenomenon, or reality, S. But M in this world of ours is inevitably conjoined with P; so that P is the next thing that we may expect to find conjoined with the fact S. We may conclude or infer P, through the intermediation of the M which our sagacity began by discerning, when S came before it, to be the essence of the case.

Now note that if P have any value or importance for us, M was a very good character for our sagacity to pounce upon and abstract. If, on the contrary, P were of no importance, some other character than M would have been a better essence for us to conceive of S by. Psychologically, as a rule, P overshadows the process from the start. We are *seeking* P, or something like P. But the bare totality of S does not yield it to our gaze; and casting about for some point in S to take hold of which will lead us to P, we hit, if we are sagacious, upon M, because M happens to be just the character which is knit up with P. . . .

Reasoning is always to attain some particular conclusion, or to gratify some special curiosity. It not only breaks up the datum placed before it and conceives it abstractly; it must conceive it *rightly* too; and conceiving it rightly means conceiving it by that one particular abstract character which leads to the one sort of conclusion which it is the reasoner's temporary interest to attain.

The *results* of reasoning may be hit upon by accident. The stereoscope was actually a result of reasoning; it is conceivable, however, that a man playing with pictures and mirrors might accidentally have hit upon it. Cats have been known to open doors by pulling latches, etc. But no cat, if the latch got out of order, could open the door again, unless some new accident of random fumbling taught her to associate some new total movement with the total phenomenon of the closed door. A reasoning man, however, would open the door by first analysing the hindrance. He would ascertain what particular feature of the door was wrong. The lever, e.g., does not raise the latch sufficiently from its slot – case of insufficient elevation: raise door bodily on hinges! Or door sticks at bottom by friction against sill: raise it bodily up! Now it is obvious that a child or an idiot might without this reasoning learn the *rule* for opening that particular door. I remember a clock which the maid-servant had discovered would not go unless it were supported so as to tilt slightly forwards. She had stumbled on this method after many weeks of groping. The reason of the stoppage was the friction of the pendulum-bob against the back of the clock-case, a reason which an educated man would have analysed out in five minutes. I have a student's lamp of which the flame vibrates most unpleasantly unless the chimney be raised about a sixteenth of an inch. I learned the remedy after much torment by accident, and now always keep the chimney up with a small wedge. But my procedure is a mere association of two totals, diseased object and remedy. One learned in pneumatics could have abstracted the *cause* of the disease, and thence inferred the remedy immediately. . . .

Thus, there are two great points in reasoning. First an extracted character is taken as equivalent to the entire datum from which it comes; and,

Second, the character thus taken suggests a certain consequence more obviously than it was suggested by the total datum as it originally came. . . .

Sagacity. To reason, then, we must be able to extract characters, — not *any* characters, but the right characters for our conclusion. If we extract the wrong character, it will not lead to that conclusion. Here, then, is the difficulty: *How are characters extracted, and why does it require the advent of a genius in many cases before the fitting character is brought to light?* Why cannot anybody reason as well as anybody else? Why does it need a Newton to notice the law of the squares, a Darwin to notice the survival of the fittest? To answer these questions we must begin a new research, and see how our insight into facts naturally grows.

All our knowledge at first is vague. When we say that

a thing is vague, we mean that it has no subdivisions *ab intra*, nor precise limitations *ab extra;* but still all the forms of thought may apply to it. ... In this vague way, probably, does the room appear to the babe who first begins to be conscious of it as something other than his moving nurse. It has no subdivisions in his mind, unless, perhaps, the window is able to attract his separate notice. In this vague way, certainly, does every entirely new experience appear to the adult. A library, a museum, a machine-shop, are mere confused wholes to the uninstructed, but the machinist, the antiquary, and the bookworm perhaps hardly notice the whole at all, so eager are they to pounce upon the details. Familiarity has in them bred discrimination.... A layman present at a shipwreck, a battle, or a fire is helpless. Discrimination has been so little awakened in him by experience that his consciousness leaves no single point of the complex situation accented and standing out for him to begin to act upon. But the sailor, the fireman, and the general know directly at what corner to take up the business. They 'see into the situation' – that is, they analyse it – with their first glance. It is full of delicately differenced ingredients which their education has little by little brought to their consciousness, but of which the novice gains no clear idea.

How this power of analysis was brought about we saw in our chapters on Discrimination and Attention. We dissociate the elements of originally vague totals by attending to them or noticing them alternately, of course. But what determines which element we shall attend to first? There are two immediate and obvious answers: first, our practical or instinctive interests; and second, our æsthetic interests. The dog singles out of any situation its smells, and the horse its sounds, because they may reveal facts of practical moment, and are instinctively exciting to these several creatures. The infant notices the candle-flame or the window, and ignores the rest of the room, because those objects give him a vivid pleasure. So, the country boy dissociates the blackberry, the chestnut, and the wintergreen, from the vague mass of other shrubs and trees, for their practical uses. . . .

Now, a creature which has few instinctive impulses, or interests practical or æsthetic, will dissociate few characters, and will, at best, have limited reasoning powers; whilst one whose interests are very varied will reason much better. Man, by his immensely varied instincts, practical wants, and æsthetic feelings, to which every sense contributes, would, by dint of these alone, be sure to dissociate vastly more characters than any other animal; and accordingly we find that the lowest savages reason incomparably better than the highest brutes. . . .

The Help given by Association by Similarity. It is probable, also, that man's *superior association by similarity* has much to do with those discriminations of character on which his higher flights of reasoning are based. As this latter is an important matter . . . it behoves me to dwell a little upon it here.

What does the reader do when he wishes to see in what the precise likeness or difference of two objects lies? He transfers his attention as rapidly as possible, backwards and forwards, from one to the other. The rapid alteration in consciousness shakes out, as it were, the points of difference or agreement, which would have slumbered forever unnoticed if the consciousness of the objects compared had occurred at widely distant periods of time. What does the scientific man do who searches for the reason or law embedded in a phenomenon? He deliberately accumulates all the instances he can find which have any analogy to that phenomenon; and, by simultaneously filling his mind with them all, he frequently succeeds in detaching from the collection the peculiarity which he was unable to formulate in one alone; even though that one had been preceded in his former experience by all of those with which he now at once confronts it. These examples show that the mere general fact of having occurred at some time in one's experience, with varying concomitants, is not by itself a sufficient reason for a character to be dissociated now. We need something more; we need that the varying concomitants should in all their variety be brought into consciousness *at once*. Not till then will the character in question escape from its adhesion to each and all of them and stand alone. This will immediately be recognized by those who have read Mill's Logic as the ground of Utility in his famous 'four methods of experimental inquiry'. . . .

Now it is obvious that any mind in which association by similarity is highly developed is a mind which will spontaneously form lists of instances like this. Take a present fact A, with a character m in it. The mind may fail at first to notice this character m at all. But if A calls up C, D, E, and F, — these being phenomena which resemble A in possessing m, but which may not have entered for months into the experience of the animal who now experiences A, why, plainly, such association performs the part of the reader's deliberately rapid comparison referred to above, and of the systematic consideration of like cases by the scientific investigator, and may lead to the noticing of m in an abstract way. Certainly this is obvious; and no conclusion is left to us but to assert that, after the few most powerful practical and æsthetic interests, our chief help towards noticing those special characters of phenomena which, when once possessed and named, are used as reasons, class names, essences, or middle terms, *is this asso-*

ciation by similarity. Without it, indeed, the deliberate procedure of the scientific man would be impossible: he could never collect his analogous instances. But it operates of itself in highly-gifted minds without any deliberation, spontaneously collecting analogous instances, uniting in a moment what in nature the whole breadth of space and time keeps separate, and so permitting a perception of identical points in the midst of different circumstances,

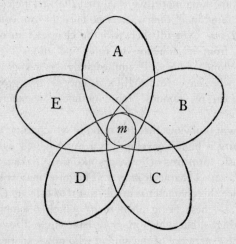

which minds governed wholly by the law of contiguity could never begin to attain.

The figure shows this. If *m*, in the present representation *A*, calls up *B*, *C*, *D*, and *E*, which are similar to *A* in possessing it, and calls them up in rapid succession, then *m*, being associated almost simultaneously with such varying concomitants, will 'roll out' and attract our separate notice.

If so much is clear to the reader, he will be willing to

admit that the mind *in which this mode of association most prevails* will, from its better opportunity of extricating characters, be the one most prone to reasoned thinking; whilst, on the other hand, a mind in which we do not detect reasoned thinking will probably be one in which association by contiguity holds almost exclusive sway.

Geniuses are, by common consent, considered to differ from ordinary minds by an unusual development of association by similarity. One of Professor Bain's best strokes of work is the exhibition of this truth. . . . But as, according to our view, there are two stages in reasoned thought, one where similarity merely *operates* to call up cognate thoughts, and another farther stage, where the bond of identity between the cognate thoughts is *noticed;* so *minds of genius may be divided into two main sorts, those who notice the bond and those who merely obey it.* The first are the abstract reasoners, properly so-called, the men of science and philosophers—the analysts, in a word; the latter are the poets, the critics – the artists, in a word, the men of intuitions. These judge rightly, classify cases, characterize them by the most striking analogic epithets, but go no farther. At first sight it might seem that the analytic mind represented simply a higher intellectual stage, and that the intuitive mind represented an arrested stage of intellectual development; but the difference is not so simple as this. Professor Bain has said that a man's advance to the scientific stage (the stage of noticing and abstracting the bond of similarity) may often be due to an *absence* of certain emotional sensibilities. The sense of colour, he says, may no less determine a mind away from science than it determines it towards painting. There must be a penury in one's interest in the details of particular forms in order to permit the forces of the intellect to be concentrated on what is common to many forms. . . . A certain richness of the æsthetic nature may, therefore, easily keep one in the intuitive stage. . . .

But although this is true, and although it would be absurd in an absolute way to say that a given analytic mind was superior to any intuitional one, yet it is none the less true that the former *represents* the higher stage. Men, taken historically, reason by analogy long before they have learned to reason by abstract characters. Association by similarity and true reasoning may have identical results. If a philosopher wishes to prove to you why you should do a certain thing, he may do so by using abstract considerations exclusively; a savage will prove the same by reminding you of a similar case in which you notoriously do as he now proposes, and this with no ability to state the *point* in which the cases are similar. In all primitive literature, in all savage oratory, we find persuasion carried on exclusively by parables and similes. . . . This is the stage in which proverbial philosophy reigns supreme. 'An empty sack can't stand straight' will stand for the reason why a man with debts may lose his honesty; and 'a bird in the hand is worth two in the bush' will serve to back up one's exhortations to prudence. Or we answer the question: 'Why is snow white?' by saying, 'For the same reason that soap-suds or whipped eggs are white' – in other words, instead of giving the *reason* for a fact, we give another *example* of the same fact. This offering a similar instance, instead of a reason, has often been criticized as one of the forms of logical depravity in men. But manifestly it is not a perverse act of thought, but only an incomplete one. Furnishing parallel cases is the necessary first step towards abstracting the reason imbedded in them all. . . .

Over immense departments of our thought we are still, all of us, in the savage state. Similarity operates in us, but abstraction has not taken place. We know what the present case is like, we know what it reminds us of, we have an intuition of the right course to take, if it be a practical matter. But analytic thought has made no tracks, and we cannot justify ourselves to others. In ethical, psychological and æsthetic matters, to give a clear reason for one's judgment is universally recognized as a mark of rare genius. The helplessness of uneducated people to account for their likes and dislikes is often ludicrous. Ask the first Irish girl why she likes this country better or worse than her home, and see how much she can tell you. But if you ask your most educated friend why he prefers Titian to Paul Veronese, you will hardly get more of a reply; and you will probably get absolutely none if you inquire why Beethoven reminds him of Michael Angelo, or how it comes that a bare figure with unduly flexed joints, by the latter, can so suggest the moral tragedy of life. His thought obeys a *nexus*, but cannot name it. And so it is with all those judgments of *experts*, which even though unmotived are so valuable. Saturated with experience of a particular class of materials, an expert intuitively feels whether a newly-reported fact is probable or not, whether a proposed hypothesis is worthless or the reverse. He instinctively knows that, in a novel case, this and not that will be the promising course of action. The well-known story of the old judge advising the new one never to give reasons for his decisions, 'the decisions will probably be right, the reasons will surely be wrong', illustrates this. The doctor will feel that the patient is doomed, the dentist will have a premonition that the tooth will break, though neither can articulate a reason for his foreboding. The reason lies imbedded, but not yet laid bare, in all the countless previous cases dimly suggested by the actual one, all calling up the same conclusion, which the adept thus finds himself swept on to, he knows not how or why. . . .

INSTINCT

Its Definition. Instinct is usually defined as the faculty of acting in such a way as to produce certain ends, without foresight of the ends, and without previous education in the performance. Instincts are the functional correlatives of structure. With the presence of a certain organ goes, one may say, almost always a native aptitude for its use.

The actions we call instinctive all conform to the general reflex type; they are called forth by determinate sensory stimuli in contact with the animal's body, or at a distance in his environment. The cat runs after the mouse, runs or shows fight before the dog, avoids falling from walls and trees, shuns fire and water, etc., not because he has any notion either of life or of death, or of self, or of preservation. He has probably attained to no one of these conceptions in such a way as to react definitely upon it. He acts in each case separately, and simply because he cannot help it; being so framed that when that particular running thing called a mouse appears in his field of vision he *must* pursue; that when that particular barking and obstreperous thing called a dog appears there he *must* retire, if at a distance, and scratch if close by; that he *must* withdraw his feet from water and his face from flame, etc. His nervous system is to a great extent a preorganized bundle of such reactions – they are as fatal as sneezing, and as exactly correlated to their special excitants as it is to its own. Although the naturalist may, for his own convenience, class these reactions under general heads, he must not forget that in the animal it is a particular sensation or perception or image which calls them forth.

At first this view astounds us by the enormous number

of special adjustments it supposes animals to possess ready-made in anticipation of the outer things among which they are to dwell. *Can* mutual dependence be so intricate and go so far? Is each thing born fitted to particular other things, and to them exclusively, as locks are fitted to their keys? Undoubtedly this must be believed to be so. Each nook and cranny of creation, down to our very skin and entrails, has its living inhabitants, with organs suited to the place, to devour and digest the food it harbours and to meet the dangers it conceals; and the minuteness of adaptation thus shown in the way of *structure* knows no bounds. Even so are there no bounds to the minuteness of adaptation in the way of *conduct* which the several inhabitants display.

The older writings on instinct are ineffectual wastes of words, because their authors never came down to this definite and simple point of view, but smothered everything in vague wonder at the clairvoyant and prophetic power of the animals – so superior to anything in man – and at the beneficence of God in endowing them with such a gift. But God's beneficence endows them, first of all, with a nervous system; and, turning our attention to this, makes instinct immediately appear neither more nor less wonderful than all the other facts of life. . . .

Now, why do the various animals do what seem to us such strange things, in the presence of such outlandish stimuli? Why does the hen, for example, submit herself to the tedium of incubating such a fearfully uninteresting set of objects as a nestful of eggs, unless she have some sort of a prophetic inkling of the result? The only answer is *ad hominem*. We can only interpret the instincts of brutes by what we know of instincts in ourselves. Why do men always lie down, when they can, on soft beds rather than on hard floors? Why do they sit round the stove on a cold day? Why, in a room, do they place themselves, ninety-nine times out of a hundred, with their faces towards its middle rather than to the wall? Why do they prefer saddle of mutton and champagne to hard-tack and ditch-water? Why does the maiden interest the youth so that everything about her seems more important and significant than anything else in the world? Nothing more can be said than that these are human ways, and that every creature *likes* its own ways, and takes to the following them as a matter of course. Science may come and consider these ways, and find that most of them are useful. But it is not for the sake of their utility that they are followed, but because at the moment of following them we feel that that is the only appropriate and natural thing to do. Not one man in a billion, when taking his dinner, ever thinks of utility. He eats because the food tastes good and makes him want more. If you ask him *why* he should want to eat more of what tastes like that, instead of revering you as a philosopher he will probably laugh at you for a fool. The connection between the savoury sensation and the act it awakens is for him absolute and *selbstverständlich*, an '*a priori* synthesis' of the most perfect sort, needing no proof but its own evidence. To the metaphysician alone can such questions occur as: Why do we smile, when pleased, and not scowl? Why are we unable to talk to a crowd as we talk to a single friend? Why does a particular maiden turn our wits so upside-down? The common man can only say, '*Of course* we smile, *of course* our heart palpitates at the sight of the crowd, *of course* we love the maiden, that beautiful soul clad in that perfect form, so palpably and flagrantly made from all eternity to be loved!'

And so, probably, does each animal feel about the particular things it tends to do in presence of particular objects. They, too, are *a priori* syntheses. To the lion it is the lioness which is made to be loved; to the bear, the she-bear. To the broody hen the notion would probably seem monstrous that there should be a creature in the world to whom a nestful of eggs was not the utterly fascinating and precious and never-to-be-too-much-sat-upon object which it is to her. . . .

Instincts are not always blind or invariable. Nothing is commoner than the remark that man differs from lower creatures by the almost total absence of instincts, and the assumption of their work in him by 'reason'. A fruitless discussion might be waged on this point by two theorizers who were careful not to define their terms. We must of course avoid a quarrel about words, and the facts of the case are really tolerably plain. Man has a far greater variety of *impulses* than any lower animal; and any one of these impulses, taken in itself, is as 'blind' as the lowest instinct can be; but, owing to man's memory, power of reflection, and power of inference, they come each one to be felt by him, after he has once yielded to them and experienced their results, in connection with a *foresight* of those results. In this condition an impulse acted out may be said to be acted out, in part at least, *for the sake* of its results. It is obvious that *every instinctive act, in an animal with memory, must cease to be 'blind' after being once repeated*, and must be accompanied with foresight of its 'end' just so far as that end may have fallen under the animal's cognizance. An insect that lays her eggs in a place where she never sees them hatched must always do so 'blindly'; but a hen who has already hatched a brood can hardly be assumed to sit with perfect 'blindness' on her second nest. Some expectation of consequences must in every case like this be aroused; and this expectation, according as it is that of something desired or of something disliked, must necessarily either re-enforce or inhibit the mere impulse. The hen's idea of the chickens would probably encourage her to sit; a rat's memory, on the other hand, of a former escape from a trap would neutralize his impulse to take bait from anything that reminded him of that trap. . . .

It is plain, then, that, *no matter how well endowed an animal may originally be in the way of instincts, his resultant actions will be much modified if the instincts combine with experience*, if in addition to impulses he have memories, associations, inferences, and expectations, on any considerable scale. An object O, on which he has an instinctive impulse to react in the manner A, would *directly* provoke him to that reaction. But O has meantime become for him a *sign* of the nearness of P, on which he has an equally strong impulse to react in the manner B, quite unlike A. So that when he meets O, the immediate impulse A and the remote impulse B struggle in his breast for the mastery. The fatality and uniformity said to be characteristic of instinctive actions will be so little manifest that one might be tempted to deny to him altogether the possession of any instinct about the object O. Yet how false this judgment would be! The instinct about O is there; only by the complication of the associative machinery it has come into conflict with another instinct about P. . . .

Wherever the mind is elevated enough to discriminate; wherever several distinct sensory elements must combine to discharge the reflex arc; wherever, instead of plumping into action instantly at the first rough intimation of what *sort* of a thing is there, the agent waits to see which *one* of its kind it is and what the *circumstances* are of its appearance; wherever different individuals and different circumstances can impel him in different ways; wherever these are the conditions — we have a masking of the elementary constitution of the instinctive life. The whole story of our dealings with the lower wild animals is the history of our taking advantage of the way in which they judge of everything by its mere label, as it were, so as to ensnare or kill them. Nature, in them, has left matters in this rough way, and made them act *always* in the manner which would be *oftenest* right. There are more worms unattached to hooks than impaled upon them; therefore, on the whole, says Nature to her fishy children, bite at *every* worm and take your chances. But as her children get higher, and their lives more precious, she reduces the risks. Since what seems to be the same object may be now a genuine food and now a bait; since in gregarious species each individual may prove to be either the friend or the rival, according to the circumstances, of another; since any entirely unknown object may be fraught with weal or woe, *Nature implants contrary impulses to act on many classes of things,* and leaves it to slight alterations in the conditions of the individual case to decide which impulse shall carry the day. Thus, greediness and suspicion, curiosity and timidity, coyness and desire, bashfulness and vanity, sociability and pugnacity, seem to shoot over into each other as quickly, and to remain in as unstable an equilibrium, in the higher birds and mammals as in man. All are impulses, congenital, blind at first, and productive of motor reactions of a rigorously determinate sort. *Each one of them then is an instinct,* as instincts are commonly defined. *But they contradict each other* — 'experience' in each particular opportunity of application usually deciding the issue. *The animal that exhibits them loses the 'instinctive' demeanour* and appears to lead a life of hesitation and choice, an intellectual life; *not, however, because he has no instincts — rather because he has so many that they block each other's path.*

Thus we may confidently say that however uncertain man's reactions upon his environment may sometimes seem in comparison with those of lower mammals, the uncertainty is probably not due to their possession of any principles of action which he lacks. *On the contrary, man possesses all the impulses that they have, and a great many more besides.* In other words, there is no material antagonism between instinct and reason. Reason, *per se*, can inhibit no impulses; the only thing that can neutralize an impulse is an impulse the other way. Reason may, however, make an *inference which will excite the imagination so as to let loose* the impulse the other way; and thus, though the animal richest in reason is also the animal richest in instinctive impulses too, he never seems the fatal automaton which a *merely* instinctive animal must be. . . .

WILL

Voluntary Acts. The movements we have studied hitherto have been automatic and reflex, and (on the first occasion of their performance, at any rate) unforeseen by the agent. The movements to the study of which we now address ourselves, being desired and intended beforehand, are of course done with full prevision of what they are to be. It follows from this that *voluntary movements must be secondary, not primary, functions of our organism.* This is the first point to understand in the psychology of Volition. Reflex, instinctive, and emotional movements are all primary performances. The nerve-centres are so organized that certain stimuli pull the trigger of certain explosive parts; and a creature going through one of these explosions for the first time undergoes an entirely novel experience. . . . But if, in voluntary action properly so called, the act must be foreseen, it follows that no creature not endowed with prophetic power can perform an act voluntarily for the first time. Well, we are no more endowed with prophetic vision of what movements lie in our power than we are endowed with prophetic vision of what sensations we are capable of receiving. As we must wait for the sensations to be given us, so we must wait for the movements to be performed involuntarily, before we can frame ideas of what either of these things are. We learn all our possibilities by the way of experience. When a particular movement, having once occurred in a random, reflex, or involuntary way, has left an image of itself in the memory, then the movement can be desired again, and deliberately willed. But it is impossible to see how it could be willed before.

A supply of ideas of the various movements that are possible, left in the memory by experiences of their involuntary performance, is thus the first prerequisite of the voluntary life.

Two Kinds of Ideas of Movement. Now these ideas may be either *resident* or *remote*. That is, they may be of the movement as it feels, when taking place, in the moving parts; or they may be of the movement as it feels in some other part of the body which it affects (strokes, presses, scratches, etc.), or as it sounds, or as it looks. . . . That 'idea of a movement' which must precede it in order that it be voluntary is the anticipation of the movement's sensible effects, resident or remote. Such anticipations, to say the least, determine *what* our movements shall be. I have [so far] spoken as if they also might determine *that* they shall be. This, no doubt, has disconcerted many readers, for it certainly seems as if a special fiat, or consent to the movement, were required in addition to the mere conception of it, in many cases of volition; and this fiat I have altogether left out of my account. This leads us to the next point in our discussion.

Ideo-motor Action. The question is this: *Is the bare idea of a movement's sensible effects its sufficient motor-cue, or must there be an additional mental antecedent, in the shape of a fiat, decision, consent, volitional mandate, or other synonymous phenomenon of consciousness, before the movement can follow?*

I answer: Sometimes the bare idea is sufficient, but sometimes an additional conscious element, in the shape of a fiat, mandate, or express consent, has to intervene and precede the movement. The cases without a fiat constitute the more fundamental, because the more simple, variety. The others involve a special complication, which must be fully discussed at the proper time. For the present let us turn to *ideo-motor action*, as it has been termed, or the sequence of movement upon the mere thought of it, without a special fiat, as the type of the process of volition.

Wherever a movement *unhesitatingly and immediately* follows upon the idea of it, we have ideo-motor action. We are then aware of nothing between the conception and the execution. All sorts of neuro-muscular processes come between, of course, but we know absolutely nothing of them. We think the act, and it is done; and that is all that introspection tells us of the matter. Dr Carpenter, who first used, I believe, the name of ideo-motor action, placed it, if I mistake not, among the curiosities of our mental life. The truth is that it is no curiosity, but simply the normal process stripped of disguise. Whilst talking I become conscious of a pin on the floor, or of some dust on my sleeve. Without interrupting the conversation I brush away the dust or pick up the pin. I make no express resolve, but the mere perception of the object and the fleeting notion of the act seem of themselves to bring the latter about. Similarly, I sit at table after dinner and find myself from time to time taking nuts or raisins out of the dish and eating them. My dinner properly is over, and in the heat of the conversation I am hardly aware of what I do; but the perception of the fruit, and the fleeting notion that I may eat it, seem fatally to bring the act about. There is certainly no express fiat here; any more than there is in all those habitual goings and comings and rearrangements of ourselves which fill every hour of the day. . . .

In all this the determining condition of the unhesitating and resistless sequence of the act seems to be *the absence of any conflicting notion in the mind*. Either there is nothing else at all in the mind, or what is there does not conflict. We know what it is to get out of bed on a freezing morning in a room without a fire, and how the very vital principle within us protests against the ordeal. Probably most persons have lain on certain mornings for an hour at a time unable to brace themselves to the resolve. We think how late we shall be, how the duties of the day will suffer; we say, 'I *must* get up, this is ignominious', etc.; but still the warm couch feels too delicious, the cold outside too cruel, and resolution faints away and postpones itself again and again just as it seemed on the verge of bursting the resistance and passing over into the decisive act. Now how do we *ever* get up under such circumstances? If I may generalize from my own experience, we more often than not get up without any struggle or decision at all. We suddenly find that we *have* got up. A fortunate lapse of consciousness occurs; we forget both the warmth and the cold; we fall into some revery connected with the day's life, in the course of which the idea flashes across us, 'Hollo! I must lie here no longer' — an idea which at that lucky instant awakens no contradictory or paralyzing suggestions, and consequently produces immediately its appropriate motor effects. It was our acute consciousness of both the warmth and the cold during the period of struggle, which paralyzed our activity then and kept our idea of rising in the condition of *wish* and not of *will*. The moment these inhibitory ideas ceased, the original idea exerted its effects.

This case seems to me to contain in miniature form the data for an entire psychology of volition. It was in fact through meditating on the phenomenon in my own person that I first became convinced of the truth of the doctrine which these pages present, and which I need here illustrate by no further examples. The reason why that doctrine is not a self-evident truth is that we have so many ideas which *do not* result in action. But it will be seen that in every such case, without exception, that is because other ideas simultaneously present rob them of their impulsive power. But even here, and when a movement is inhibited from *completely* taking place by contrary ideas, it will *incipiently* take place. To quote Lotze:

'The spectator accompanies the throwing of a billiard-ball, or the thrust of the swordsman, with slight movements of his arm; the untaught narrator tells his story with many gesticulations; the reader while absorbed in the perusal of a battle-scene feels a slight tension run through his muscular system, keeping time as it were with the actions he is reading of'. . . .

The 'willing-game', the exhibitions of so-called 'mind-reading', or more properly muscle-reading, which have lately grown so fashionable, are based on this incipient obedience of muscular contraction to idea, even when the deliberate intention is that no contraction shall occur.

We may then lay it down for certain that *every representation of a movement awakens in some degree the actual movement which is its object; and awakens it in a maximum degree whenever it is not kept from so doing by an antagonistic representation present simultaneously to the mind.*

The express fiat, or act of mental consent to the movement, comes in when the neutralization of the antagonistic and inhibitory idea is required. But that there is no express fiat needed when the conditions are simple, the reader ought now to be convinced. Lest, however, he should still share the common prejudice that voluntary action without 'exertion of will-power' is Hamlet with the prince's part left out, I will make a few further remarks. The first point to start from, in understanding voluntary action and the possible occurrence of it with no fiat or express resolve, is the fact that consciousness is *in its very nature impulsive.* We do not first have a sensation or thought, and then have to *add* something dynamic to it to get a movement. Every pulse of feeling which we have is the correlate of some neural activity that is already on its way to instigate a movement. . . . The popular notion that consciousness is not essentially a forerunner of activity, but that the latter must result from some superadded 'will-force', is a very natural inference from those special cases in which we think of an act for an indefinite length of time without the action taking place. These cases, however, are not the norm; they are cases of inhibition by antagonistic thoughts. When the blocking is released we feel as if an inward spring were let loose, and this is the additional impulse or *fiat* upon which the act effectively succeeds. *Movement is the natural immediate effect of the process of feeling, irrespective of what the quality of the feeling may be. It is so in reflex action, it is so in emotional expression, it is so in the voluntary life.* Ideo-motor action is thus no paradox, to be softened or explained away. It obeys the type of all conscious action, and from it one must start to explain the sort of action in which a special fiat is involved. . . .

The theory of ideo-motor action has recently received strong experimental confirmation, through the development of apparatus which can detect minute changes of electrical potential in nerve and muscle fibres. Such electrical changes, it is now realized, occur in all muscular activity, even when the muscular contractions are so slight as to be undetectable by ordinary methods; and the changes can be amplified and recorded by attaching electrodes to the subject's body in the neighbourhood of the muscles concerned, and connecting the electrodes with a highly sensitive galvanometer.

In an experiment carried out by Jacobson,[7] the subject lay relaxed on a couch in a darkened room with electrodes attached to the arm muscles. He was then told to imagine himself performing various actions, such as lifting a weight or throwing a ball. In every case, marked galvanometer deflections were observed soon after the instruction was given. The subject was unable to imagine the movements without the deflections occurring. Similar results were obtained from the eye muscles, when the subject was told to call up visual images, and from the tongue and lip muscles when he was told to imagine himself counting, or speaking to a friend.

Action after Deliberation. We are now in a position to describe *what happens in deliberate action*, or when the mind has many objects before it, related to each other in antagonistic or in favourable ways. One of these objects of its thought may be an act. By itself this would prompt a movement; some of the additional objects or considerations, however, block the motor discharge, whilst others, on the contrary, solicit it to take place. The result is that

7. Cf. Crafts, L. W., and others, *Recent Experiments in Psychology* (1938), pp. 371-7.

peculiar feeling of inward unrest known as *indecision*.
Fortunately it is too familiar to need description, for to
describe it would be impossible. As long as it lasts, with the
various objects before the attention, we are said to *deliberate*; and when finally the original suggestion either
prevails and makes the movement take place, or gets
definitively quenched by its antagonists, we are said to
decide, or to *utter our voluntary fiat*, in favour of one or the
other course. The reinforcing and inhibiting objects meanwhile are termed the *reasons* or *motives* by which the decision is brought about. . . .

The deliberation may last for weeks or months, occupying at intervals the mind. The motives which yesterday
seemed full of urgency and blood and life to-day feel
strangely weak and pale and dead. But as little to-day as
to-morrow is the question finally resolved. Something tells
us that all this is provisional; that the weakened reasons
will wax strong again, and the stronger weaken; that
equilibrium is unreached; that testing our reasons, not
obeying them, is still the order of the day, and that we must
wait awhile, patiently or impatiently, until our mind is
made up 'for good and all.' . . .

The decision may come in either of many modes. I
will try briefly to sketch the most characteristic types of it,
merely warning the reader that this is only an introspective account of symptoms and phenomena, and that
all questions of causal agency, whether neural or spiritual,
are relegated to a later page.

Five Chief Types of Decision. Turning now to the form
of the decision itself, we may distinguish five chief types.
The first may be called the reasonable type. It is that of
those cases in which the arguments for and against a given
course seem gradually and almost insensibly to settle
themselves in the mind and to end by leaving a clear

balance in favour of one alternative, which alternative we then adopt without effort or constraint. Until this rational balancing of the books is consummated we have a calm feeling that the evidence is not yet all in, and this keeps action in suspense. But some day we wake with the sense that we see the matter rightly, that no new light will be thrown on it by further delay, and that it had better be settled *now*. In this easy transition from doubt to assurance we seem to ourselves almost passive; the 'reasons' which decide us appearing to flow in from the nature of things, and to owe nothing to our will. We have, however, a perfect sense of being *free*, in that we are devoid of any feeling of coercion. The conclusive reason for the decision in these cases usually is the discovery that we can refer the case to a *class* upon which we are accustomed to act unhesitatingly in a certain stereotyped way. . . .

In action as in reasoning, then, the great thing is the quest of the right conception. The concrete dilemmas do not come to us with labels gummed upon their backs. We may name them by many names. The wise man is he who succeeds in finding the name which suits the needs of the particular occasion best (p. 140 ff.). A 'reasonable' character is one who has a store of stable and worthy ends, and who does not decide about an action till he has calmly ascertained whether it be ministerial or detrimental to any one of these.

In the next two types of decision, the final fiat occurs before the evidence is all 'in'. It often happens that no paramount and authoritative reason for either course will come. Either seems a good, and there is no umpire to decide which should yield its place to the other. We grow tired of long hesitation and inconclusiveness, and the hour may come when we feel that even a bad decision is better than no decision at all. Under these conditions it will often happen that some accidental circumstance, supervening at a particular moment upon our mental weariness, will upset the balance in the direction of one of the alternatives, to which then we feel ourselves committed, although an opposite accident at the same time might have produced the opposite result.

In the *second type* our feeling is to a great extent that of letting ourselves drift with a certain indifferent acquiescence in a direction accidentally determined *from without*, with the conviction that, after all, we might as well stand by this course as by the other, and that things are in any event sure to turn out sufficiently right.

In the *third type* the determination seems equally accidental, but it comes from within, and not from without. It often happens, when the absence of imperative principle is perplexing and suspense distracting, that we find ourselves acting, as it were, automatically, and as if by a spontaneous discharge of our nerves, in the direction of one of the horns of the dilemma. But so exciting is this sense of motion after our intolerable pent-up state that we eagerly throw ourselves into it. 'Forward now!' we inwardly cry, 'though the heavens fall'. This reckless and exultant espousal of an energy so little premeditated by us that we feel rather like passive spectators cheering on the display of some extraneous force than like voluntary agents is a type of decision too abrupt and tumultuous to occur often in humdrum and cool-blooded natures. But it is probably frequent in persons of strong emotional endowment and unstable or vacillating character. And in men of the world-shaking type, the Napoleons, Luthers, etc., in whom tenacious passion combines with ebullient activity, when by any chance the passion's outlet has been dammed by scruples or apprehensions, the resolution is probably often of this catastrophic kind. The flood breaks quite unexpectedly through the dam. That it should so often do so is quite sufficient to account for the tendency of these characters to a fatalistic mood of mind. And the fatalistic mood itself is sure to reinforce the strength of the energy just started on its exciting path of discharge.

There is a *fourth form* of decision, which often ends deliberation as suddenly as the third form does. It comes when, in consequence of some outer experience or some inexplicable inward change, *we suddenly pass from the easy and careless to the sober and strenuous mood*, or possibly the other way. The whole scale of values of our motives and impulses then undergoes a change like that which a change of the observer's level produces on a view. The most sobering possible agents are objects of grief and fear. When one of these affects us, all 'light fantastic' notions lose their motive power, all solemn ones find theirs multiplied many-fold. The consequence is an instant abandonment of the more trivial projects with which we had been dallying, and an instant practical acceptance of the more grim and earnest alternative which till then could not extort our mind's consent. All those 'changes of heart', 'awakenings of conscience', etc., which make new men of so many of us may be classed under this head. The character abruptly rises to another 'level', and deliberation comes to an immediate end.

In the *fifth and final type* of decision, the feeling that the evidence is all in, and that reason has balanced the books, may be either present or absent. But in either case we feel, in deciding, as if we ourselves by our own wilful act inclined the beam: in the former case by adding our living effort to the weight of the logical reason which, taken alone, seems powerless to make the act discharge; in the latter by a kind of creative contribution of something instead of a reason which does a reason's work. The slow dead heave of the will that is felt in these instances makes of them a class altogether different subjectively from all the four preceding classes. What the heave of the will betokens metaphysically, what the effort might lead us to infer about a will-power distinct from motives, are not matters that concern us yet. Subjectively and phenomenally, the *feeling of effort*, absent from the former decisions, accompanies these. Whether it be the dreary resignation for the sake of austere and naked duty of all sorts of rich mundane delights; or whether it be the heavy resolve that of two mutually exclusive trains of future fact, both sweet and good and with no strictly objective or imperative principle of choice between them, one shall forevermore become impossible, while the other shall become reality; it is a desolate and acrid sort of act, an entrance into a lonesome moral wilderness. If examined closely, its chief difference from the former cases appears to be that in those cases the mind at the moment of deciding on the triumphant alternative dropped the other one wholly or nearly out of sight, whereas here both alternatives are steadily held in view, and in the very act of murdering the vanquished possibility the chooser realizes how much in that instant he is making himself lose. It is deliberately driving a thorn into one's flesh; and the sense of *inward effort* with which the act is accompanied is an element which sets this fifth type of decision in strong contrast with the previous four varieties, and makes of it an altogether peculiar sort of mental phenomenon. . . .

The existence of the effort as a phenomenal fact in our consciousness cannot of course be doubted or denied. Its significance, on the other hand, is a matter about which the gravest difference of opinion prevails. Questions as momentous as that of the very existence of spiritual causality, as vast as that of universal predestination or freewill, depend on its interpretation. It therefore becomes essential that we study with some care the conditions under which the feeling of volitional effort is found.

Healthiness of Will. There is a certain normal ratio in the impulsive power of different mental objects, which characterizes what may be called ordinary healthiness of will, and which is departed from only at exceptional times or by exceptional individuals. The states of mind which normally possess the most impulsive quality are either those which represent objects of passion, appetite, or emotion – objects of instinctive reaction, in short; or they are feelings or ideas of pleasure or of pain; or ideas which for any reason we have grown accustomed to obey, so that the habit of reacting on them is ingrained; or finally, in comparison with ideas of remoter objects, they are ideas of objects present or near in space and time. Compared with these various objects, all far-off considerations, all highly abstract conceptions, unaccustomed reasons, and motives foreign to the instinctive history of the race, have little or no impulsive power. They prevail, when they ever do prevail, *with effort; and the normal,* as distinguished from the pathological, *sphere of effort is thus found wherever non-instinctive motives to behaviour must be reinforced so as to rule the day. . . .*

Effort feels like an original force. [The feeling of effort, in other words, occurs] whenever a rarer and more ideal impulse is called upon to neutralize others of a more instinctive and habitual kind; it does so whenever strongly explosive tendencies are checked, or strongly obstructive conditions overcome. . . . Now our spontaneous way of conceiving the effort, under all these circumstances, is as an active force adding its strength to that of the motives which ultimately prevail. When outer forces impinge upon a body, we say that the resultant motion is in the line of least resistance, or of greatest traction. But it is a curious fact that our spontaneous language never speaks of volition with effort in this way. Of course if we proceed *a priori* and define the line of least resistance as the line that is followed, the physical law must also hold good in the mental sphere. But we *feel*, in all hard cases of volition, as if the line taken, when the rarer and more ideal motives prevail, were the line of greater resistance, and as if the line of coarser motivation were the more pervious and easy one, even at the very moment when we refuse to follow it. He who under the surgeon's knife represses cries of pain, or he who exposes himself to social obloquy for duty's sake, feels as if he were following the line of greatest temporary resistance. He speaks of conquering and overcoming his impulses and temptations.

But the sluggard, the drunkard, the coward, never talk of their conduct in that way, or say they resist their energy, overcome their sobriety, conquer their courage, and so forth. If in general we class all springs of action as propensities on the one hand and ideals on the other, the sensualist never says of his behaviour that it results from a victory over his ideals, but the moralist always speaks of his as a victory over his propensities. The sensualist uses terms of inactivity, says he forgets his ideals, is deaf to duty, and so forth; which terms seem to imply that the ideal motives *per se* can be annulled without energy or effort, and that the strongest mere traction lies in the line of the propensities. The ideal impulse appears, in comparison with this, a still small voice which must be artificially reinforced to prevail. Effort is what reinforces it, making things seem as if, while the force of propensity were essentially a fixed quantity, the ideal force might be of various amount. But what determines the amount of the effort when, by its aid, an ideal motive becomes victorious over a great sensual resistance? The very greatness of the resistance itself. If the sensual propensity is small, the effort is small. The latter is *made great* by the presence of a great antagonist to overcome. And if a brief definition of ideal or moral action were required, none could be given which would better fit the appearances than this: *It is action in the line of the greatest resistance.*

The facts may be most briefly symbolized thus, P standing for the propensity, I for the ideal impulse, and E for the effort:

$$I \; per \; se < P.$$
$$I + E > P.$$

In other words, if E adds itself to I, P immediately offers the least resistance, and motion occurs in spite of it.

But the E does not seem to form an integral part of the I. It appears adventitious and indeterminate in advance. We can make more or less as we please, and *if* we make enough we can convert the greatest mental resistance into the least. Such, at least, is the impression which the facts spontaneously produce upon us. But we will not discuss the truth of this impression at present; let us rather continue our descriptive detail. . . .

What holds attention determines action. If one must have a single name for the condition upon which the impulsive and inhibitive quality of objects depends, one had better call it their *interest.* 'The interesting' is a title which covers not only the pleasant and the painful, but also the morbidly fascinating, the tediously haunting, and even the simply habitual, inasmuch as the attention usually travels on habitual lines, and what-we-attend-to and what-interests-us are synonymous terms. It seems as if we ought to look for the secret of an idea's impulsiveness, not in any peculiar relations which it may have with paths of motor discharge, — for *all* ideas have relations with some such paths, – but rather in a preliminary phenomenon, the *urgency, namely, with which it is able to compel attention and dominate in consciousness.* Let it once so dominate, let no other ideas succeed in displacing it, and whatever motor effects belong to it by nature will inevitably occur – its impulsion, in short, will be given to boot, and will manifest itself as a matter of course. This is what we have seen in instinct, in emotion, in common ideo-motor action, in hypnotic suggestion [and] in morbid impulsion . . . the impelling idea is simply the one which possesses the attention. It is the same where pleasure and pain are the motor spurs – they drive other thoughts from consciousness at the same time that they instigate their own characteristic 'volitional' effects. And this is also what happens at the moment of the *fiat*, in all the five types of 'decision' which we have described. In short, one does not see any case in which the steadfast occupancy of consciousness does not appear to be the prime condition of impulsive power. It is still more obviously the prime condition of inhibitive power. What checks our impulses is the mere thinking of reasons to the contrary – it is their bare presence to the mind which gives the veto, and makes acts, otherwise seductive, impossible to perform. If we could only *forget* our scruples, our doubts, our fears, what exultant energy we should for a while display!

Will is a relation between the mind and its 'ideas'. In closing in, therefore, after all these preliminaries, upon the more *intimate* nature of the volitional process, we find ourselves driven more and more exclusively to consider the conditions which make ideas prevail in the mind. With the prevalence, once there as a fact, of the motive idea, the *psychology* of volition properly stops. The movements which ensue are exclusively physiological phenomena, following according to physiological laws upon the neural events to which the idea corresponds. . . . In a word, volition is a psychic or moral fact pure and simple, and is absolutely completed when the stable state of the idea is there. The supervention of motion is a supernumerary phenomenon depending on executive ganglia whose function lies outside the mind. If the ganglia work duly, the act occurs perfectly. If they work, but work wrongly, we have St Vitus's dance, locomotor ataxy, motor aphasia, or minor degrees of awkwardness. If they don't work at all, the act fails altogether, and we say the man is paralysed. He may make a tremendous effort, and contract the other muscles of the body, but the paralysed limb fails to move. In all these cases, however, the volition considered as a psychic process is intact.

Volitional effort is effort of attention. We thus find that *we reach the heart of our inquiry into volition when we ask by what process it is that the thought of any given action comes to prevail stably in the mind.* Where thoughts prevail without effort, we have sufficiently studied in the several chapters on Sensation, Association, and Attention, the laws of their advent before consciousness and of their stay. We shall not go over that ground again, for we know that interest and association are the words, let their worth be what it may, on which our explanations must perforce rely. Where, on the other hand, the prevalence of the thought is accompanied by the phenomenon of effort, the case is much less clear. Already in the chapter on Attention we postponed the final consideration of voluntary attention with effort to a later place. We have now brought things to a point at which we see that attention with effort is all that any case of volition implies. *The essential achievement of the will, in short, when it is most 'voluntary', is to attend to a difficult object and hold it fast before the mind.* The so-doing *is* the *fiat;* and it is a mere physiological incident that when the object is thus attended to, immediate motor consequences should ensue.

Effort of attention is thus the essential phenomenon of will. Every reader must know by his own experience that this is so, for every reader must have felt some fiery passion's grasp. What constitutes the difficulty for a man labouring under an unwise passion of acting as if the passion were wise? Certainly there is no physical difficulty. It is as easy physically to avoid a fight as to begin one, to pocket one's money as to squander it on one's cupidities, to walk away from as towards a coquette's door. The difficulty is mental: it is that of getting the idea of the wise action to stay before our mind at all. When any strong emotional state whatever is upon us, the tendency is for no images but such as are congruous with it to come up. If others by chance offer themselves, they are instantly smothered and crowded out. If we be joyous, we cannot keep thinking of those uncertainties and risks of failure which abound upon our path; if lugubrious, we cannot think of new triumphs, travels, loves, and joys; nor if vengeful, of our oppressor's community of nature with ourselves. The cooling advice which we get from others when the fever-fit is on us is the most jarring and exasperating thing in life. Reply we cannot, so we get angry; for by a sort of self-preserving instinct which our passion has, it feels that these chill objects, if they once but gain a lodgment, will work and work until they have frozen the very vital spark from out of all our mood and brought our airy castles in ruin to the ground. Such is the inevitable effect of reasonable ideas over others – *if they can once get a quiet hearing;* and passion's cue accordingly is always and everywhere to prevent their still small voice from being heard at all. 'Let me not think of that! Don't speak to me of that!' This is the sudden cry of all those who in a passion perceive some sobering considerations about to check them in mid-career. There is something so icy in this cold-water bath, something which seems so hostile to the movement of our life, so purely negative, in Reason, when she lays her corpse-like finger on our heart and says, 'Halt! give up! leave off! go back! sit down!' that it is no wonder that to most men the steadying influence seems, for the time being, a very minister of death.

The strong-willed man, however, is the man who hears the still small voice unflinchingly, and who, when the death-bringing consideration comes, looks at its face, consents to its presence, clings to it, affirms it, and holds it fast, in spite of the host of exciting mental images which rise in revolt against it and would expel it from the mind. Sustained in this way by a resolute effort of attention, the difficult object ere long begins to call up its own congeners and associates and ends by changing the disposition of the man's consciousness altogether. And with his consciousness his action changes, for the new object, once stably in possession of the field of his thoughts, infallibly produces its own motor effects. The difficulty lies in the gaining possession of that field. Though the spontaneous drift of thought is all the other way, the attention must be kept strained on that one object until at last it *grows*, so as to maintain itself before the mind with ease. This strain of the attention is the fundamental act of will. And the will's work is in most cases practically ended when the bare presence to our thought of the naturally unwelcome object has been secured. For the mysterious tie between the thought and the motor centres next comes into play, and, in a way which we cannot even guess at, the obedience of the bodily organs follows as a matter of course.

In all this one sees how the immediate point of application of the volitional effort lies exclusively in the mental world. The whole drama is a mental drama. The whole difficulty is a mental difficulty, a difficulty with an ideal object of our thought. It is, in one word, an *idea* to which our will applies itself, an idea which if we let it go would slip away, but which we will not let go. *Consent to the idea's undivided presence, this is effort's sole achievement.* Its only function is to get this feeling of consent into the mind. And for this there is but one way. The idea to be consented to must be kept from flickering and going out. It must be held steadily before the mind until it *fills* the mind. Such filling of the mind by an idea, with its congruous associates, *is* consent to the idea and to the fact which the idea represents. If the idea be that, or include that, of a bodily movement of our own, then we call the consent thus laboriously gained a motor volition. For Nature here 'backs' us instantaneously and follows up our inward willingness by outward changes on her own part. She does this in no other instance. Pity she should not have been more generous, nor made a world whose other parts were as immediately subject to our will!

On p. 164, in describing the 'reasonable type' of decision, it was said that it usually came when the right conception of the case was found. Where, however, the right conception is an anti-impulsive one, the whole intellectual ingenuity of the man usually goes to work to crowd it out of sight, and to find for the emergency names by the help of which the dispositions of the moment may sound sanctified, and sloth or passion may reign unchecked. How many excuses does the drunkard find when each new temptation comes! It is a new brand of liquor which the interests of intellectual culture in such matters oblige him to test; moreover it is poured out and it is sin to waste it; also others are drinking and it would be churlishness to refuse. Or it is but to enable him to sleep, or just to get through this job of work; or it isn't drinking, it is because he feels so cold; or it is Christmas-day; or it is a means of stimulating him to make a more powerful resolution in favour of abstinence than any he has hitherto made; or it is just this once, and once doesn't count, etc., etc., *ad libitum* – it is, in fact, anything you like except *being a drunkard. That is* the conception that will not stay before the poor soul's attention. But if he once gets able to pick out that way of conceiving, from all the other possible ways of conceiving the various opportunities which occur, if through thick and thin he holds to it that this is being a drunkard and is nothing else, he is not likely to remain one long. The effort by which he succeeds in keeping the right *name* unwaveringly present to his mind proves to be his saving moral act. . . .

To sum it all up in a word, *the terminus of the psychological process in volition, the point to which the will is directly applied, is always an idea.* There are at all times *some* ideas from which we shy away like frightened horses the moment we get a glimpse of their forbidding profile upon the threshold of our thought. *The only resistance which our will can possibly experience is the resistance which such an idea offers to being attended to at all.* To attend to it is the volitional act, and the only inward volitional act which we ever perform.

The Question of 'Free-will'. As was remarked on p. 170, in the experience of effort we feel as if we might make more or less than we actually at any moment are making.

The effort appears, in other words, not as a fixed reaction on our part which the object that resists us necessarily calls forth, but as what the mathematicians call an 'independent variable' amongst the fixed data of the case, our motives, character, etc. If it be really so, if the amount of our effort is not a determinate function of those other data, then, in common parlance, *our wills are free.* If, on the contrary, the amount of effort be a fixed function, so that whatever object at any time fills our consciousness was from eternity bound to fill it then and there, and compel from us the exact effort, neither more nor less, which we bestow upon it, — then our wills are not free, and all our acts are foreordained. *The question of fact in the free-will controversy is thus extremely simple. It relates solely to the amount of effort of attention which we can at any time put forth.* Are the duration and intensity of this effort fixed functions of the object, or are they not? Now, as I just said, it *seems* as if we might exert more or less in any given case. When a man has let his thoughts go for days and weeks until at last they culminate in some particularly dirty or cowardly or cruel act, it is hard to persuade him, in the midst of his remorse, that he might not have reined them in; hard to make him believe that this whole goodly universe (which his act so jars upon) required and exacted it of him at that fatal moment, and from eternity made aught else impossible. But, on the other hand, there is the certainty that all his *effortless* volitions are resultants of interests and associations whose strength and sequence are mechanically determined by the structure of that physical mass, his brain; and the general continuity of things and the monistic conception of the world may lead one irresistibly to postulate that a little fact like effort can form no real exception to the overwhelming reign of deterministic law. Even in effortless volition we have the consciousness of the alternative being also possible. This is surely a delusion here; why is it not a delusion everywhere? . . .

Professor Lipps, in his admirably clear deterministic statement, so far from admitting that the feeling of effort testifies to an increment of force exerted, explains it as a sign that force is lost. We speak of effort, according to him, whenever a force expends itself (wholly or partly) in neutralizing another force, and so fails of its own possible outward effect. . . . Where the forces are ideas, both sets of them, strictly speaking, are the seat of effort — both those which tend to explode and those which tend to check them. We, however, call the more abundant mass of ideas *ourselves;* and talking of its effort as *our* effort, and of that of the smaller mass of ideas as the *resistance*, we say that our effort sometimes overcomes the resistances offered by the inertias of an obstructed, and sometimes those presented by the impulsions of an explosive, will. Really both effort and resistance are ours, and the identification of our *self* with one of these factors is an illusion and a trick of speech. I do not see how anyone can fail . . . to recognize the fascinating simplicity of some such view as his. Nor do I see why *for scientific purposes* one need give it up even if indeterminate amounts of effort really do occur. . . .

The fact is that the question of free-will is insoluble on strictly psychologic grounds. After a certain amount of effort of attention has been given to an idea, it is manifestly impossible to tell whether either more or less of it *might* have been given or not. To tell that, we should have to ascend to the antecedents of the effort, and defining them with mathematical exactitude, prove, by laws of which we have not at present even an inkling, that the only amount of sequent effort which could *possibly* comport with them was the precise amount that actually came. Such measurements, whether of psychic or of neural quantities, and such deductive reasonings as this method of proof implies, will surely be forever beyond human reach. No serious psychologist or physiologist will venture even to suggest a notion of how they might be practically made. Had one no motives drawn from elsewhere to make one partial to either solution, one might easily leave the matter undecided. But a psychologist cannot be expected to be thus impartial, having a great motive in favour of determinism. He wants to build a *Science;* and a Science is a system of fixed relations. Wherever there are independent variables, there Science stops. So far, then, as our volitions may be independent variables, a scientific psychology must ignore that fact, and treat of them only so far as they are fixed functions. In other words, she must deal with the *general laws* of volition exclusively; with the impulsive and inhibitory character of ideas; with the nature of their appeals to the attention; with the conditions under which effort may arise, etc.; but not with the precise amounts of effort, for these, if our wills be free, are impossible to compute. She thus abstracts from free-will, without necessarily denying its existence. Practically, however, such abstraction is not distinguished from rejection; and most actual psychologists have no hesitation in denying that free-will exists.

For ourselves, we can hand the free-will controversy over to metaphysics. Psychology will surely never grow refined enough to discover, in the case of any individual's decision, a discrepancy between her scientific calculations and the fact. Her prevision will never foretell, whether the effort be completely predestinate or not, the way in which each individual emergency is resolved. Psychology will be psychology, and Science science, as much as ever (as much and no more) in this world, whether free-will be true in it or not.

We can thus ignore the free-will question in psychology. As we said on p. 175, the operation of free effort, if it existed, could only be to hold some one ideal object, or part of an object, a little longer or a little more intensely before the mind. Amongst the alternatives which present themselves as *genuine possibles*, it would thus make one effective. And although such quickening of one idea might be morally and historically momentous, yet, if considered *dynamically*, it would be an operation amongst those physiological infinitesimals which an actual science must forever neglect.

THE VARIETIES OF

RELIGIOUS EXPERIENCE

The Varieties of Religious Experience

CIRCUMSCRIPTION OF THE TOPIC

As regards the manner in which I shall have to administer this lectureship, I am neither a theologian, nor a scholar learned in the history of religions, nor an anthropologist. Psychology is the only branch of learning in which I am particularly versed. To the psychologist the religious propensities of man must be at least as interesting as any other of the facts pertaining to his mental constitution. It would seem, therefore, that, as a psychologist, the natural thing for me would be to invite you to a descriptive survey of those religious propensities. . . .

In these lectures I propose to ignore the institutional branch entirely, to say nothing of the ecclesiastical organization, to consider as little as possible the systematic theology and the ideas about the gods themselves, and to confine myself as far as I can to personal religion pure and simple. . . . Religion, therefore, as I now ask you arbitrarily to take it, shall mean for us *the feelings, acts, and experiences of individual men in their solitude, so far as they apprehend themselves to stand in relation to whatever they may consider the divine.*

RELIGION AND PSYCHOPATHOLOGY

THERE are many religious persons . . . who may . . . feel at first a little startled at the purely existential point of view from which in the following lectures the phenomena of religious experience must be considered. When I handle them biologically and psychologically as if they were mere curious facts of individual history, some of you may think it a degradation of so sublime a subject, and may even suspect me, until my purpose gets more fully expressed, of deliberately seeking to discredit the religious side of life.

Such a result is of course absolutely alien to my intention; and since such a prejudice on your part would seriously obstruct the due effect of much of what I have to relate, I will devote a few more words to the point.

There can be no doubt that as a matter of fact a religious life, exclusively pursued, does tend to make the person exceptional and eccentric. I speak not now of your ordinary religious believer, who follows the conventional observances of his country, whether it be Buddhist, Christian, or Mohammedan. His religion has been made for him by others, communicated to him by tradition, determined to fixed forms by imitation, and retained by habit. It would profit us little to study this second-hand religious life. We must make search rather for the original experiences which were the pattern-setters to all this mass of suggested feeling and imitated conduct. These experiences we can only find in individuals for whom religion exists not as a dull habit, but as an acute fever rather. But such individuals are 'geniuses' in the religious line; and like many other geniuses who have brought forth fruits effective enough for commemoration in the pages of biography, such religious geniuses have often shown symptoms of nervous instability. Even more perhaps than other kinds of genius, religious leaders have been subject to abnormal psychical visitations. Invariably they have been creatures of exalted emotional sensibility. Often they have led a discordant inner life, and had melancholy during a part of their career. They have known no measure, been liable to obsessions and fixed ideas; and frequently they have fallen into trances, heard voices, seen visions, and presented all sorts of peculiarities which are ordinarily classed as pathological. Often, moreover, these pathological features in their career have helped to give them their religious authority and influence. . . .

Bent as we are on studying religion's existential conditions, we cannot possibly ignore these pathological aspects of the subject. We must describe and name them just as if they occurred in non-religious men. It is true that we instinctively recoil from seeing an object to which our emotions and affections are committed handled by the intellect as any other object is handled. The first thing the intellect does with an object is to class it along with something else. But any object that is infinitely important to us and awakens our devotion feels to us also as if it must be *sui generis* and unique. Probably a crab would be filled with a sense of personal outrage if it could hear us class it without ado or apology as a crustacean, and thus dispose of it. 'I am no such thing,' it would say; 'I am MYSELF, MYSELF alone.'

The next thing the intellect does is to lay bare the causes in which the thing originates. Spinoza . . . remarks that he will consider our passions and their properties with the same eye with which he looks on all other natural things, since the consequences of our affections flow from their nature with the same necessity as it results from the nature of a triangle that its three angles should be equal to two right angles. Similarly M. Taine, in the introduction to his history of English literature, has written: 'Whether facts be moral or physical, it makes no matter. They always have their causes. There are causes for ambition, courage, veracity, just as there are for digestion, muscular movement, animal heat. Vice and virtue are products like vitriol and sugar.' When we read such proclamations of the intellect bent on showing the existential conditions of absolutely everything, we feel — quite apart from our legitimate impatience at the somewhat ridiculous swagger of the programme, in view of what the authors are actually able to perform — menaced and negated in the springs of our innermost life. Such cold-blooded assimilations threaten, we think, to undo our soul's vital secrets, as if the same breath which should succeed in explaining their origin would simultaneously explain away their significance, and make them appear of no more preciousness, either, than the useful groceries of which M. Taine speaks.

Perhaps the commonest expression of this assumption that spiritual value is undone if lowly origin be asserted is seen in those comments which unsentimental people so often pass on their more sentimental acquaintances ... Fanny's extraordinary conscientiousness is merely a matter of over-instigated nerves ... William's melancholy about the universe is due to bad digestion — probably his liver is torpid. ... Peter would be less troubled about his soul if he would take more exercise in the open air, etc. A more fully developed example of the same kind of reasoning is the fashion, quite common nowadays among certain writers, of criticizing the religious emotions by showing a connection between them and the sexual life. Conversion is a crisis of puberty and adolescence. The macerations of saints, and the devotion of missionaries, are only instances of the parental instinct of self-sacrifice gone astray. For the hysterical nun, starving for natural life, Christ is but an imaginary substitute for a more earthly object of affection. And the like.[1]

1. As with many ideas that float in the air of one's time, this notion shrinks from dogmatic general statement and expresses itself only partially and by innuendo. It seems to me that few conceptions are less instructive than this re-interpretation of religion as perverted sexuality. It reminds one, so crudely is it often employed, of the famous Catholic taunt, that the Reformation may be best understood by remembering that its *fons et origo* was Luther's wish to

We are surely all familiar in a general way with this method of discrediting states of mind for which we have an antipathy. We all use it to some degree in criticizing persons whose state of mind we regard as overstrained. But when other people criticize our own more exalted soul-flights by calling them 'nothing but' expressions of our organic disposition, we feel outraged and hurt, for we know that, whatever be our organism's peculiarities, our mental states have their substantive value as revelations of the living truth; and we wish that all this medical materialism could be made to hold its tongue.

Medical materialism seems indeed a good appellation for the too simple-minded system of thought which we are considering. Medical materialism finishes up Saint Paul by

marry a nun: — the effects are infinitely wider than the alleged causes, and for the most part opposite in nature. It is true that in the vast collection of religious phenomena, some are undisguisedly amatory — e.g. sex-deities and obscene rites in polytheism, and ecstatic feeling of union with the Saviour in a few Christian mystics. But then why not equally call religion an aberration of the digestive function, and prove one's point by the worship of Bacchus and Ceres, or by the ecstatic feelings of some other saints about the Eucharist? Religious language clothes itself in such poor symbols as our life affords, and the whole organism gives overtones of comment whenever the mind is strongly stirred to expression. Language drawn from eating and drinking is probably as common in religious literature as is language drawn from sexual life. We 'hunger and thirst' after righteousness; we 'find the Lord a sweet savour'; we 'taste and see that he is good'. . . .

. . . These arguments are as good as much of the reasoning one hears in favour of the sexual theory. But the champions of the latter will then say that their chief argument has no analogue elsewhere. The two main phenomena of religion, namely, melancholy and conversion, they will say, are essentially phenomena of adolescence, and therefore synchronous with the development of sexual life. To which the retort again is easy. Even were the asserted synchrony unrestrictedly true as a fact (which it is not), it is not only the sexual life, but the entire higher mental life which awakens during adolescence. One might then as well set up the thesis that the interest in mechanics, physics, chemistry, logic, philosophy, and sociology, which springs up during adolescent years along with that in poetry and religion, is also a perversion of the sexual instinct.

calling his vision on the road to Damascus a discharging lesion of the occipital cortex, he being an epileptic. It snuffs out Saint Teresa as an hysteric, Saint Francis of Assisi as an hereditary degenerate ... Carlyle's organ-tones of misery it accounts for by a gastro-duodenal catarrh. All such mental over-tensions, it says, are, when you come to the bottom of the matter, mere affairs of diathesis (auto-intoxications most probably), due to the perverted action of various glands which physiology will yet discover.

And medical materialism then thinks that the spiritual authority of all such personages is successfully undermined.

Let us ourselves look at the matter in the largest possible way. Modern psychology, finding definite psycho-physical connections to hold good, assumes as a convenient hypothesis that the dependence of mental states upon bodily conditions must be thorough-going and complete. If we adopt the assumption, then of course what medical materialism insists on must be true in a general way, if not in every detail: Saint Paul certainly had once an epileptoid, if not an epileptic seizure; ... Carlyle was undoubtedly auto-intoxicated by some organ or other, no matter which, — and the rest. But now, I ask you, how can such an existential account of facts of mental history decide in one way or another upon their spiritual significance? According to the general postulate of psychology just referred to, there is not a single one of our states of mind, high or low, healthy or morbid, that has not some organic process as its condition. Scientific theories are organically conditioned just as much as religious emotions are; and if we only knew the facts intimately enough, we should doubtless see 'the liver' determining the dicta of the sturdy atheist as decisively as it does those of the Methodist under conviction anxious about his soul. ... So of all our raptures and our drynesses, our longings and pantings, our questions and beliefs. They are equally organically founded, be they of religious or of non-religious content.

To plead the organic causation of a religious state of mind, then, in refutation of its claim to possess superior spiritual value, is quite illogical and arbitrary, unless one has already worked out in advance some psycho-physical theory connecting spiritual values in general with determinate sorts of physiological change. Otherwise none of our thoughts and feelings, not even our scientific doctrines, not even our *dis*-beliefs, could retain any value as revelations of the truth, for every one of them without exception flows from the state of their possessor's body at the time.

It is needless to say that medical materialism draws in point of fact no such sweeping sceptical conclusion. It is sure, just as every simple man is sure, that some states of mind are inwardly superior to others, and reveal to us more truth, and in this it simply makes use of an ordinary spiritual judgment. It has no physiological theory of the production of these its favourite states, by which it may accredit them; and its attempt to discredit the states which it dislikes, by vaguely associating them with nerves and liver, and connecting them with names connoting bodily affliction, is altogether illogical and inconsistent.

Let us play fair in this whole matter, and be quite candid with ourselves and with the facts. When we think certain states of mind superior to others, is it ever because of what we know concerning their organic antecedents? No! it is always for two entirely different reasons. It is either because we take an immediate delight in them; or else it is because we believe them to bring us good consequential fruits for life. When we speak disparagingly of 'feverish fancies', surely the fever-process as such is not the ground of our dis-esteem — for aught we know to the contrary, 103° or 104° Fahrenheit might be a much more favourable temperature for truths to germinate and sprout in, than the more ordinary blood-heat of 97° or 98°. It is either the disagreeableness itself of the fancies, or their inability to bear the criticisms of the convalescent hour. . . .

What immediately feels most 'good' is not always most 'true', when measured by the verdict of the rest of experience. The difference between Philip drunk and Philip sober is the classic instance in corroboration. If merely 'feeling good' could decide, drunkenness would be the supremely valid human experience. But its revelations, however acutely satisfying at the moment, are inserted into an environment which refuses to bear them out for any length of time. The consequence of this discrepancy of the two criteria is the uncertainty which still prevails over so many of our spiritual judgments. There are moments of sentimental and mystical experience – we shall hereafter hear much of them – that carry an enormous sense of inner authority and illumination with them when they come. But they come seldom, and they do not come to everyone; and the rest of life makes either no connection with them, or tends to contradict them more than it confirms them. Some persons follow more the voice of the moment in these cases, some prefer to be guided by the average results. Hence the sad discordancy of so many of the spiritual judgments of human beings; a discordancy which will be brought home to us acutely enough before these lectures end.

[James then discusses current theories of the instability of genius, and continues:] There is of course no special affinity between crankiness as such and superior intellect, for most psychopaths have feeble intellects, and superior intellects more commonly have normal nervous systems. But the psychopathic temperament, whatever be the intellect with which it finds itself paired, often brings with it ardour and excitability of character. The cranky person has extraordinary emotional susceptibility. He is liable to fixed ideas and obsessions. His conceptions tend to pass immediately into belief and action; and when he gets a new idea, he has no rest till he proclaims it, or in some way 'works it off'. 'What shall I think of it?' a common person says to himself about a vexed question; but in a 'cranky' mind 'What must I do about it?' is the form the question tends to take. In the autobiography of that high-souled woman, Mrs Annie Besant, I read the following passage: 'Plenty of people wish well to any good cause, but very few care to exert themselves to help it, and still fewer will risk anything in its support. "Some one ought to do it, but why should I?" is the ever re-echoed phrase of weak-kneed amiability. "Some one ought to do it, so why not I?" is the cry of some earnest servant of man, eagerly forward springing to face some perilous duty. Between these two sentences lie whole centuries of moral evolution.' True enough! and between these two sentences lie also the different destinies of the ordinary sluggard and the psychopathic man. Thus, when a superior intellect and a psychopathic temperament coalesce — as in the endless permutations and combinations of human faculty, they are bound to coalesce often enough — in the same individual, we have the best possible condition for the kind of effective genius that gets into the biographical dictionaries. . . .

In the psychopathic temperament we have the emotionality which is the *sine qua non* of moral perception; we have the intensity and tendency to emphasis which are the essence of practical moral vigour; and we have the love of metaphysics and mysticism which carry one's interests beyond the surface of the sensible world. What, then, is more natural than that this temperament should introduce one to regions of religious truth, to corners of the universe, which your robust Philistine type of nervous system, forever offering its biceps to be felt, thumping its breast, and thanking Heaven that it hasn't a single morbid fibre in its composition, would be sure to hide forever from its self-satisfied possessors?

If there were such a thing as inspiration from a higher realm, it might well be that the neurotic temperament would furnish the chief condition of the requisite receptivity. And having said thus much, I think that I may let the matter of religion and neuroticism drop.

THE RELIGION OF HEALTHY-MINDEDNESS

IN the hour immediately before us, I shall invite you to consider the simpler kinds of religious happiness, leaving the more complex sorts to be treated on a later day.

In many persons, happiness is congenital and irreclaimable. 'Cosmic emotion' inevitably takes in them the form of enthusiasm and freedom. I speak not only of those who are animally happy. I mean those who, when unhappiness is offered or proposed to them, positively refuse to feel it, as if it were something mean and wrong. We find such persons in every age, passionately flinging themselves upon their sense of the goodness of life, in spite of the hardships of their own condition, and in spite of the sinister theologies into which they may be born. . . . It is probable that there never has been a century in which the deliberate refusal to think ill of life has not been idealized by a number of persons. . . . Saint Francis and his immediate disciples were, on the whole, of this company of spirits, of which there are of course infinite varieties. Rousseau in the earlier years of his writing, Diderot, B. de Saint Pierre, and many of the leaders of the eighteenth-century anti-christian movement were of this optimistic type. They owed their influence to a certain authoritativeness in their feeling that Nature, if you will only trust her sufficietlny, is absolutely good.

The supreme contemporary example of such an inability to feel evil is of course Walt Whitman. . . . A passionate and mystic ontological emotion suffuses his words, and ends by persuading the reader that men and women, life and death, and all things are divinely good.

Thus it has come about that many persons to-day regard Walt Whitman as the restorer of the eternal natural religion. He has infected them with his own love of comrades, with his own gladness that he and they exist. Societies are actually formed for his cult; . . . hymns are written in his peculiar prosody; and he is even explicitly compared with the founder of the Christian religion, not altogether to the advantage of the latter.

Whitman is often spoken of as a 'pagan'. The word nowadays means sometimes the mere natural animal man without a sense of sin; sometimes it means a Greek or Roman with his own peculiar religious consciousness. In neither of these senses does it fitly define this poet. He is more than your mere animal man who has not tasted of the tree of good and evil. He is aware enough of sin for a swagger to be present in his indifference towards it, a conscious pride in his freedom from flexions and contractions, which your genuine pagan in the first sense of the word would never show. . . .

. . . But on the other hand Whitman is less than a Greek or a Roman; for their consciousness, even in Homeric times, was full to the brim of the sad mortality of this sunlit world, and such a consciousness Walt Whitman resolutely refuses to adopt. When, for example, Achilles, about to slay Lycaon, Priam's young son, hears him sue for mercy, he stops to say:

Ah, friend, thou too must die: why thus lamentest thou? Patroclos too is dead, who was better far than thou. . . . Over me too hang death and forceful fate. There cometh morn or eve or some noonday when my life too some man shall take in battle, whether with spear he smite, or arrow from the string.

Then Achilles savagely severs the poor boy's neck with his sword, heaves him by the foot into the Scamander, and calls to the fishes of the river to eat the white fat of Lycaon. Just as here the cruelty and the sympathy each ring true, and do not mix or interfere with one another, so did the Greeks and Romans keep all their sadnesses and gladnesses unmingled and entire. Instinctive good they did not reckon sin; nor had they any such desire to save the credit of the universe as to make them insist, as so many of *us* insist, that what immediately appears as evil must be 'good in the making,' or something equally ingenious. Good was good, and bad just bad, for the earlier Greeks. They neither denied the ills of nature, — Walt Whitman's verse 'What is called good is perfect and what is called bad is just as perfect,' would have been mere silliness to them, — nor did they, in order to escape from those ills, invent 'another and a better world' of the imagination, in which, along with the ills, the innocent goods of sense would also find no place. This integrity of the instinctive reactions, this freedom from all moral sophistry and strain, gives a pathetic dignity to ancient pagan feeling.[2] And this quality Whitman's outpourings have not got. His optimism is too

2. [Editor's footnote.] Santayana (who was a pupil of James) consciously or unconsciously echoed this passage in the comments on Homer which he put into the mouth of the hero of *The Last Puritan*. 'Homer is merciless, covers up nothing, adds nothing, simply tells you the awful truth. Yet he walks on the sunny side of the world: its tragedy in sunlight, despair at high noon, death in the bloom of youth. And you feel that the sun will keep on shining just the same, and that the next morning will be just as beautiful, and just as cruel. Homer accepted things as they have to be, felt the beauty of them, and didn't indulge in any hocus pocus to explain the horror away.'

voluntary and defiant; his gospel has a touch of bravado
and an affected twist, and this diminishes its effect on many
readers who yet are well disposed towards optimism, and
on the whole quite willing to admit that in important
respects Whitman is of the genuine lineage of the prophets.

If, then, we give the name of healthy-mindedness to the
tendency which looks on all things and sees that they are
good, we find that we must distinguish between a more
involuntary and a more voluntary or systematic way of
being healthy-minded. In its involuntary variety, healthy-
mindedness is a way of feeling happy about things immediately. In its systematical variety, it is an abstract way of
conceiving things as good. Every abstract way of conceiving things selects some one aspect of them as their essence
for the time being, and disregards the other aspects.
Systematic healthy-mindedness, conceiving good as the
essential and universal aspect of being, deliberately
excludes evil from its field of vision; and although, when
thus nakedly stated, this might seem a difficult feat to
perform for one who is intellectually sincere with himself
and honest about facts, a little reflection shows that the
situation is too complex to lie open to so simple a criticism.

In the first place, happiness, like every other emotional
state, has blindness and insensibility to opposing facts given
it as its instinctive weapon for self-protection against
disturbance. . . . To the man actively happy, from whatever
cause, evil simply cannot then and there be believed in.
He must ignore it; and to the bystander he may then seem
perversely to shut his eyes to it and hush it up.

But more than this: this hushing of it up may, in a
perfectly candid and honest mind, grow into a deliberate
religious policy or *parti pris*. Much of what we call evil
is due entirely to the way men take the phenomenon. It
can so often be converted into a bracing and tonic good by

a simple change of the sufferer's inner attitude from one of fear to one of fight. ... Refuse to admit [its] badness; despise [its] power; ignore [its] presence; turn your attention the other way; and so far as you yourself are concerned at any rate, though the facts may still exist, their evil character exists no longer. ...

The deliberate adoption of an optimistic turn of mind thus makes its entrance into philosophy. And once in, it is hard to trace its lawful bounds. Not only does the human instinct for happiness, bent on self-protection by ignoring, keep working in its favour, but higher inner ideals have weighty words to say. The attitude of unhappiness is not only painful, it is mean and ugly. What can be more base and unworthy than the pining, puling, mumping mood, no matter by what outward ills it may have been engendered? What is more injurious to others? What less helpful as a way out of the difficulty? It but fastens and perpetuates the trouble which occasioned it, and increases the total evil of the situation. At all costs, then, we ought to reduce the sway of that mood; we ought to scout it in ourselves and others, and never show it tolerance. But it is impossible to carry on this discipline in the subjective sphere without zealously emphasizing the brighter and minimizing the darker aspects of the objective sphere of things at the same time. And thus our resolution not to indulge in misery, beginning at a comparatively small point within ourselves, may not stop until it has brought the entire frame of reality under a systematic conception optimistic enough to be congenial with its needs. ...

The systematic cultivation of healthy-mindedness as a religious attitude is therefore consonant with important currents in human nature, and is anything but absurd. In fact, we all do cultivate it more or less, even when our professed theology should in consistency forbid it. We divert our attention from disease and death as much as we can; and the slaughter-houses and indecencies without end on which our life is founded are huddled out of sight and never mentioned, so that the world we recognize officially in literature and in society is a poetic fiction far handsomer and cleaner and better than the world that really is.[3]

The advance of liberalism, so-called, in Christianity, during the past fifty years, may fairly be called a victory of healthy-mindedness within the church over the morbidness with which the old hell-fire theology was more harmoniously related. We have now whole congregations whose preachers . . . insist on the dignity rather than on the depravity of man. They look at the continual preoccupation of the old-fashioned Christian with the salvation of his soul as something sickly and reprehensible rather than admirable; and a sanguine and 'muscular' attitude, which to our forefathers would have seemed purely heathen, has become in their eyes an ideal element of Christian character. I am not asking whether or not they are right. I am only pointing out the change.

The persons to whom I refer have still retained for the most part their nominal connection with Christianity, in spite of their discarding of its more pessimistic theological elements. But in that 'theory of evolution' which, gathering momentum for a century, has within the past twenty-five years swept so rapidly over Europe and America, we see the ground laid for a new sort of religion of Nature, which has entirely displaced Christianity from the thought of a large part of our generation. The idea of a universal evolution lends itself to a doctrine of general meliorism and progress which fits the religious needs of the

---

3. [Editor's footnote.] The Californian cemeteries described by Evelyn Waugh in *The Loved One* perhaps indicate the high-water-mark of this tendency.

healthy-minded so well that it seems almost as if it might have been created for their use. Accordingly we find 'evolutionism' interpreted thus optimistically and embraced as a substitute for the religion they were born in, by a multitude of our contemporaries who have either been trained scientifically, or been fond of reading popular science, and who had already begun to be inwardly dissatisfied with what seemed to them the harshness and irrationality of the orthodox Christian scheme. . . .

THE SICK SOUL

LET us now say good-bye for a while to all this way of thinking, and turn towards those persons who cannot so swiftly throw off the burden of the consciousness of evil, but are congenitally fated to suffer from its presence. Just as we saw that in healthy-mindedness there are shallower and profounder levels, happiness like that of the mere animal, and more regenerate sorts of happiness, so also are there different levels of the morbid mind, and the one is much more formidable than the other. There are people for whom evil means only a mal-adjustment with *things*, a wrong correspondence of one's life with the environment. Such evil as this is curable, in principle at least, upon the natural plane. . . . But there are others for whom evil is no mere relation of the subject to particular outer things, but something more radical and general, a wrongness or vice in his essential nature, which no alteration of the environment, or any superficial rearrangement of the inner self, can cure, and which requires a supernatural remedy. On the whole, the Latin races have leaned more towards the former way of looking upon evil, as made up of ills and sins in the plural, removable in detail; while the Germanic races have tended rather to think of Sin in the singular, and with a capital S, as of something ineradicably ingrained in our natural subjectivity, and never to be removed by any superficial piecemeal operations. . . .

We must now address ourselves to the unpleasant task of hearing what the sick souls, as we may call them in contrast to the healthy-minded, have to say of the secrets of their prison-house, their own peculiar form of consciousness. Let us then resolutely turn our backs on the once-born and their sky-blue optimistic gospel; let us not simply cry out, in spite of all appearances, 'Hurrah for the Universe! – God's in his Heaven, all's right with the world'. Let us see rather whether pity, pain, and fear, and the sentiment of human helplessness may not open a profounder view and put into our hands a more complicated key to the meaning of the situation.

[James then gives various examples, both normal and pathological, of vivid awareness of the reality of evil, and continues:] Let sanguine healthy-mindedness do its best with its strange power of living in the moment and ignoring and forgetting, still the evil background is really there to be thought of, and the skull will grin in at the banquet. . . . [Thus] we can see how great an antagonism may naturally arise between the healthy-minded way of viewing life and the way that takes all this experience of evil as something essential. To this latter way, the morbid-minded way, as we might call it, healthy-mindedness pure and simple seems unspeakably blind and shallow. To the healthy-minded way, on the other hand, the way of the sick soul seems unmanly and diseased. With their grubbing in rat-holes instead of living in the light; with their manufacture of fears, and preoccupation with every unwholesome kind of misery, there is something almost obscene about these children of wrath and cravers of a second birth. If religious intolerance and hanging and burning could again become the order of the day, there is little doubt that, however it may have been in the past, the healthy-minded would at present show themselves the less indulgent party of the two.

In our own attitude, not yet abandoned, of impartial onlookers, what are we to say of this quarrel? It seems to me that we are bound to say that morbid-mindedness ranges over the wider scale of experience, and that its survey is the one that overlaps. The method of averting one's attention from evil, and living simply in the light of good, is splendid as long as it will work. It will work with many persons; it will work far more generally than most of us are ready to suppose; and within the sphere of its successful operation there is nothing to be said against it as a religious solution. But it breaks down impotently as soon as melancholy comes; and even though one be quite free from melancholy one's self, there is no doubt that healthy-mindedness is inadequate as a philosophical doctrine, because the evil facts which it refuses positively to account for are a genuine portion of reality; and they may after all be the best key to life's significance, and possibly the only openers of our eyes to the deepest levels of truth.

The normal process of life contains moments as bad as any of those which insane melancholy is filled with, moments in which radical evil gets its innings and takes its solid turn. The lunatic's visions of horror are all drawn from the material of daily fact. Our civilization is founded on the shambles, and every individual existence goes out in a lonely spasm of helpless agony. . . . Here on our very hearths and in our gardens the infernal cat plays with the panting mouse, or holds the hot bird fluttering in her jaws. Crocodiles and rattlesnakes and pythons are at this moment vessels of life as real as we are; . . . and whenever they or other wild beasts clutch their living prey, the deadly horror which an agitated melancholiac feels is the literally right reaction on the situation.

It may indeed be that no religious reconciliation with the absolute totality of things is possible. Some evils, indeed, are ministerial to higher forms of good; but it may be that there are forms of evil so extreme as to enter into no good system whatsoever, and that, in respect of such evil, dumb submission or neglect to notice is the only practical resource. This question must confront us on a later day. But provisionally, and as a mere matter of programme and method, since the evil facts are as genuine parts of nature as the good ones, the philosophic presumption should be that they have some ... significance, and that systematic healthy-mindedness, failing as it does to accord to sorrow, pain, and death any positive and active attention whatever, is formally less complete than systems that try at least to include these elements in their scope.

THE VALUE OF SAINTLINESS

[In the chapter on 'Saintliness' James quotes, and comments upon, many accounts of the lives of individual saints. He then continues:] Our survey of the phenomena of saintliness has unquestionably produced in your minds an impression of extravagance. Is it necessary, some of you have asked, as one example after another came before us, to be quite so fantastically good as that? We who have no vocation for the extremer ranges of sanctity will surely be let off at the last day if our humility, asceticism, and devoutness prove of a less convulsive sort. This practically amounts to saying that much that it is legitimate to admire in this field need nevertheless not be imitated, and that religious phenomena, like all other human phenomena, are subject to the law of the golden mean. ...

'Resist not evil', 'Love your enemies', these are saintly maxims of which men of this world find it hard to speak without impatience. Are the men of this world right, or are the saints in possession of the deeper range of truth?

No answer is possible. Here, if anywhere, one feels the complexity of the moral life, and the mysteriousness of the way in which facts and ideals are interwoven. . . .

It has often been supposed, and even now, I think, it is supposed by most persons, that there can be one intrinsically ideal type of human character. A certain kind of man, it is imagined, must be the best man absolutely and apart from the utility of his function, apart from economical considerations. The saint's type, and the knight's or gentleman's type, have always been rival claimants of this absolute ideality; and in the ideal of military religious orders both types were in a manner blended. According to the empirical philosophy, however, all ideals are matters of relation. It would be absurd, for example, to ask for a definition of 'the ideal horse', so long as dragging drays and running races, bearing children, and jogging about with tradesmen's packages all remain as indispensable differentiations of equine function. You may take what you call a general all-round animal as a compromise, but he will be inferior to any horse of a more specialized type, in some one particular direction. We must not forget this now when, in discussing saintliness, we ask if it be an ideal type of manhood. . . .

Perfect conduct is a relation between three terms: the actor, the objects for which he acts, and the recipients of the action. . . . The best intention will fail if it either work by false means or address itself to the wrong recipient. . . . As there is no worse lie than a truth misunderstood by those who hear it, so reasonable arguments, challenges to magnanimity, and appeals to sympathy or justice, are folly when we are dealing with human crocodiles and boa-constrictors. The saint may simply give the universe into the hands of the enemy by his trustfulness. He may by non-resistance cut off his own survival.

Herbert Spencer tells us that the perfect man's conduct will appear perfect only when the environment is perfect: to no inferior environment is it suitably adapted. We may paraphrase this by cordially admitting that saintly conduct would be the most perfect conduct conceivable in an environment where all were saints already; but by adding that in an environment where few are saints, and many the exact reverse of saints; it must be ill-adapted. We must frankly confess, then, using our empirical common sense and ordinary practical prejudices, that in the world that actually is, the virtues of sympathy, charity, and non-resistance may be, and often have been, manifested in excess. The powers of darkness have systematically taken advantage of them. The whole modern scientific organi-zation of charity is a consequence of the failure of simply giving alms. The whole history of constitutional govern-ment is a commentary on the excellence of resisting evil, and when one cheek is smitten, of smiting back and not turning the other cheek also.

You will agree to this in general, for in spite of the Gospel, in spite of Quakerism, in spite of Tolstoy, you believe in fighting fire with fire, in shooting down usurpers, locking up thieves, and freezing out vagabonds and swindlers.

And yet you are sure, as I am sure, that were the world confined to these hard-headed, hard-hearted, and hard-fisted methods exclusively, were there no one prompt to help a brother first, and find out afterwards whether he were worthy; no one willing to drown his private wrongs in pity for the wronger's person; no one ready to be duped many a time rather than live always on suspicion; no one glad to treat individuals passionately and impulsively rather than by general rules of prudence; the world would be an infinitely worse place than it is now to live in. The tender grace, not of a day that is dead, but of a day yet to be born somehow, with the golden rule grown natural, would be cut out from the perspective of our imaginations.

The saints, existing in this way, may, with their extravagances of human tenderness, be prophetic. Nay, innumerable times they have proved themselves prophetic. Treating those whom they met, in spite of the past, in spite of all appearances, as worthy, they may have stimulated them to *be* worthy, miraculously transformed them by their radiant example and by the challenge of their expectation.

From this point of view we may admit the human charity which we find in all saints, and the great excess of it which we find in some saints, to be a genuinely creative social force, tending to make real a degree of virtue which it alone is ready to assume as possible. . . . The saints . . . are the great torch-bearers of this belief, the tip of the wedge, the clearers of the darkness. . . . The world is not yet with them, so they often seem in the midst of the world's affairs to be preposterous. Yet they are impregnators of the world, vivifiers and animaters of potentialities of goodness which but for them would lie forever dormant. It is not possible to be quite as mean as we naturally are, when they have passed before us. One fire kindles another; and without that over-trust in human worth which they show, the rest of us would lie in spiritual stagnancy.

Momentarily considered, then, the saint may waste his tenderness and be the dupe and victim of his charitable fever, but the general function of his charity in social evolution is vital and essential. If things are ever to move upward, someone must be ready to take the first step, and assume the risk of it. No one who is not willing to try charity, to try non-resistance as the saint is always willing, can tell whether these methods will or will not succeed. When they do succeed, they are far more powerfully successful than force or worldly prudence. Force destroys enemies; and the best that can be said of prudence is that it keeps what we already have in safety. But non-resistance, when successful, turns enemies into friends; and charity regenerates its objects. These saintly methods are, as I said, creative energies; and genuine saints find in the elevated excitement with which their faith endows them an authority and impressiveness which makes them irresistible in situations where men of shallower nature cannot get on at all without the use of worldly prudence. This practical proof that worldly wisdom may be safely transcended is the saint's magic gift to mankind. . . . He is an effective ferment of goodness, a slow transmuter of the earthly into a more heavenly order. . . .

But if we turn from the abstract question to the actual situation, we find that the individual saint may be well or ill adapted, according to particular circumstances. There is, in short, no absoluteness in the excellence of sainthood. It must be confessed that as far as this world goes, anyone who makes an out-and-out saint of himself does so at his peril. If he is not a large enough man, he may appear more insignificant and contemptible, for all his saintship, than if he had remained a worldling. Accordingly religion has seldom been so radically taken in our Western world that the devotee could not mix it with some worldly temper. It has always found good men who could follow most of its impulses, but who stopped short when it came to nonresistance. Christ himself was fierce upon occasion. Cromwells, Stonewall Jacksons, Gordons, show that Christians can be strong men also.

MYSTICISM

ONE may say truly, I think, that personal religious experience has its root and centre in mystical states of consciousness; so for us, who in these lectures are treating personal experience as the exclusive subject of our study, such states of consciousness ought to form the vital chapter from which the other chapters get their light. Whether my treatment of mystical states will shed more light or darkness, I do not know, for my own constitution shuts me out from their enjoyment almost entirely, and I can speak of them only at second hand. But though forced to look upon the subject so externally, I will be as objective and receptive as I can; and I think I shall at least succeed in convincing you of the reality of the states in question, and of the paramount importance of their function.

First of all, then, I ask, What does the expression 'mystical states of consciousness' mean? How do we part off mystical states from other states?

The words 'mysticism' and 'mystical' are often used as terms of mere reproach, to throw at any opinion which we regard as vague and vast and sentimental, and without a base in either facts or logic. . . . Employed in this way the word has little value: there are too many less ambiguous synonyms. So, to keep it useful by restricting it, I will do what I did in the case of the word 'religion', and simply propose to you four marks which, when an experience has them, may justify us in calling it mystical for the purpose of the present lectures. . . .

(1) *Ineffability.* The handiest of the marks by which I classify a state of mind as mystical is negative. The subject of it immediately says that it defies expression, that no adequate report of its contents can be given in words. It

follows from this that its quality must be directly experienced; it cannot be imparted or transferred to others. In this peculiarity mystical states are more like states of feeling than like states of intellect. No one can make clear to another who has never had a certain feeling, in what the quality or worth of it consists. One must have musical ears to know the value of a symphony; one must have been in love oneself to understand a lover's state of mind. Lacking the heart or ear, we cannot interpret the musician or the lover justly, and are even likely to consider him weak-minded or absurd. The mystic finds that most of us accord to his experiences an equally incompetent treatment.

(2) *Noetic quality.* Although so similar to states of feeling, mystical states seem to those who experience them to be also states of knowledge. They are states of insight into depths of truth unplumbed by the discursive intellect. They are illuminations, revelations, full of significance and importance, all inarticulate though they remain; and as a rule they carry with them a curious sense of authority for after-time.

These two characters will entitle any state to be called mystical, in the sense in which I use the word. Two other qualities are less sharply marked, but are usually found. These are:

(3) *Transiency.* Mystical states cannot be sustained for long. Except in rare instances, half an hour, or at most an hour or two, seems to be the limit beyond which they fade into the light of common day. . . .

(4) *Passivity.* Although the oncoming of mystical states may be facilitated by preliminary voluntary operations, as by fixing the attention, or going through certain bodily performances, or in other ways which manuals of mysticism prescribe; yet when the characteristic sort of consciousness once has set in, the mystic feels as if his own will were in

abeyance, and indeed sometimes as if he were grasped and held by a superior power. . . .

Our next step should be to gain acquaintance with some typical examples. . . .

The simplest rudiment of mystical experience would seem to be that deepened sense of the significance of a maxim or formula which occasionally sweeps over one. 'I've heard that said all my life,' we exclaim, 'but I never realized its full meaning until now.' . . . This sense of deeper significance is not confined to rational propositions. Single words, and conjunctions of words, effects of light on land and sea, odours and musical sounds, all bring it when the mind is tuned aright. Most of us can remember the strangely moving power of passages in certain poems read when we were young, irrational doorways as they were through which the mystery of fact, the wildness and the pang of life, stole into our hearts and thrilled them. The words have now perhaps become mere polished surfaces for us; but lyric poetry and music are alive and significant only in proportion as they fetch these vague vistas of a life continuous with our own, beckoning and inviting, yet ever eluding our pursuit. We are alive or dead to the eternal inner message of the arts according as we have kept or lost this mystical susceptibility.

A more pronounced step forward on the mystical ladder is found in an extremely frequent phenomenon, that sudden feeling, namely, which sometimes sweeps over us, of having 'been here before', as if at some indefinite past time, in just this place, with just these people, we were already saying just these things. As Tennyson writes:

> Moreover, something is or seems,
> That touches me with mystic gleams,
> Like glimpses of forgotten dreams —

> Of something felt, like something here;
> Of something done, I know not where;
> Such as no language may declare.

Sir James Crichton-Browne has given the technical name of 'dreamy states' to these sudden invasions of vaguely reminiscent consciousness. . . .

Somewhat deeper plunges into mystical consciousness are met with in yet other dreamy states. Such feelings as these which Charles Kingsley describes are surely far from being uncommon, especially in youth:

> When I walk in the fields, I am oppressed now and then with an innate feeling that everything I see has a meaning, if I could but understand it. And this feeling of being surrounded with truths which I cannot grasp amounts to indescribable awe sometimes. . . . Have you not felt that your real soul was imperceptible to your mental vision, except in a few hallowed moments? . . .

The next step into mystical states carries us into a realm that public opinion and ethical philosophy have long since branded as pathological, though private practice and certain lyric strains of poetry seem still to bear witness to its ideality. I refer to the consciousness produced by intoxicants and anæsthetics, especially by alcohol. The sway of alcohol over mankind is unquestionably due to its power to stimulate the mystical faculties of human nature. . . . Sobriety diminishes, discriminates and says no; drunkenness expands, unites and says yes. It is, in fact, the great exciter of the *Yes* function in man. . . . To the poor and the unlettered it stands in the place of symphony concerts and of literature; and it is part of the deeper mystery and tragedy of life that whiffs and gleams of something that we immediately recognize as excellent should be vouchsafed to so many of us only in the fleeting earlier phases of what in its totality is so degrading a poisoning. The drunken consciousness is one bit of the mystic consciousness, and our total opinion of it must find its place in our opinion of that larger whole.

Nitrous oxide and ether, especially nitrous oxide, when sufficiently diluted with air, stimulate the mystical consciousness in an extraordinary degree. Depth beyond depth of truth seems revealed to the inhaler. This truth fades out, however, or escapes, at the moment of coming to; and if any words remain over in which it seemed to clothe itself, they prove to be the veriest nonsense. Nevertheless, the sense of a profound meaning having been there persists; and I know more than one person who is persuaded that in the nitrous oxide trance we have a genuine metaphysical revelation.

Some years ago I myself made some observations on this aspect of nitrous oxide intoxication, and reported them in print.[4] . . . Looking back on my own experiences, they all converge towards a kind of insight to which I cannot help ascribing some metaphysical significance. The keynote of it is invariably a reconciliation. It is as if the opposites of the world, whose contradictoriness and conflict make all our difficulties and troubles, were melted into unity. Not only do they, as contrasted species, belong to one and the same genus, but *one of the species*, the nobler and better one, *is itself the genus, and so soaks up and absorbs its opposite into*

4. [Editor's footnote.] The report is contained in an appendix to an article 'On Some Hegelisms' first published in *Mind* and reprinted in *The Will to Believe*. James there records a number of phrases dictated or written during nitrous oxide intoxication – phrases which are nonsense to the waking mind, but which at the time 'produced a delirium of theoretic rapture'. The most coherent and articulate sentence was 'There are no differences but differences of degree between different degrees of difference and no difference'. James scandalized the Hegelians by remarking that this phrase had 'the true Hegelian ring' – adding, 'But for the assurance of a certain amount of respect from them [i.e. the Hegelians] I should hardly have ventured to print what must be such caviare to the general'.

itself. This is a dark saying, I know, when thus expressed in terms of common logic, but I cannot wholly escape from its authority. I feel as if it must mean something, something like what the hegelian philosophy means, if one could only lay hold of it more clearly. Those who have ears to hear, let them hear; to me the living sense of its reality only comes in the artificial mystic state of mind. . . .

My next task is to inquire whether we can invoke the mystical experience as authoritative. Does it furnish any *warrant for the truth* for the twice-bornness and super-naturality and pantheism which it favours? I must give my answer to this question as concisely as I can.

In brief my answer is this, – and I will divide it into three parts:

(1) Mystical states, when well developed, usually are, and have the right to be, absolutely authoritative over the individuals to whom they come.

(2) No authority emanates from them which should make it a duty for those who stand outside of them to accept their revelations uncritically.

(3) They break down the authority of the non-mystical or rationalistic consciousness, based upon the understanding and the senses alone. They show it to be only one kind of consciousness. They open out the possibility of other orders of truth, in which, so far as anything in us vitally responds to them, we may freely continue to have faith.

I will take up these points one by one.

(1) As a matter of psychological fact, mystical states of a well-pronounced and emphatic sort *are* usually authoritative over those who have them. They have been 'there', and know. It is vain for rationalism to grumble about this. If the mystical truth that comes to a man proves to be a force that he can live by, what mandate have we of the majority to order him to live in another way? We can

throw him into a prison or a madhouse, but we cannot change his mind — we commonly attach it only the more stubbornly to its beliefs. It mocks our utmost efforts, as a matter of fact, and in point of logic it absolutely escapes our jurisdiction. Our own more 'rational' beliefs are based on evidence exactly similar in nature to that which mystics quote for theirs. Our senses, namely, have assured us of certain states of fact; but mystical experiences are as direct perceptions of fact for those who have them as any sensations ever were for us. The records show that even though the five senses be in abeyance in them, they are absolutely sensational in their epistemological quality, if I may be pardoned the barbarous expression, — that is, they are face to face presentations of what seems immediately to exist.

The mystic is, in short, *invulnerable*, and must be left, whether we relish it or not, in undisturbed enjoyment of his creed. Faith, says Tolstoy, is that by which men live. And faith-state and mystic state are practically convertible terms.

(2) But I now proceed to add that mystics have no right to claim that we ought to accept the deliverance of their peculiar experiences, if we are ourselves outsiders and feel no private call thereto. The utmost they can ever ask of us in this life is to admit that they establish a presumption. They form a consensus and have an unequivocal outcome; and it would be odd, mystics might say, if such a unanimous type of experience should prove to be altogether wrong. At bottom, however, this would only be an appeal to numbers, like the appeal of rationalism the other way; and the appeal to numbers has no logical force. If we acknowledge it, it is for 'suggestive', not for logical reasons: we follow the majority because to do so suits our life.

But even this presumption from the unanimity of

mystics is far from being strong. In characterizing mystic states as pantheistic, optimistic, etc., I am afraid I over-simplified the truth. I did so for expository reasons, and to keep the closer to the classic mystical tradition. The classic religious mysticism, it now must be confessed, is only a 'privileged case'. It is an *extract*, kept true to type by the selection of the fittest specimens and their preservation in 'schools'. It is carved out from a much larger mass; and if we take the larger mass as seriously as religious mysticism has historically taken itself, we find that the supposed unanimity largely disappears. To begin with, even religious mysticism itself, the kind that accumulates traditions and makes schools, is much less unanimous than I have allowed. It has been both ascetic and antinomianly self-indulgent within the Christian church. It is dualistic in Sankhya, and monistic in Vedanta philosophy. I called it pantheistic; but the great Spanish mystics are anything but pantheists. ... How different again, apart from the happiness common to all, is the mysticism of Walt Whitman, Edward Carpenter, Richard Jefferies, and other naturalistic pantheists, from the more distinctively Christian sort. The fact is that the mystical feeling of enlargement, union, and emancipation has no specific intellectual content whatever of its own. It is capable of forming matrimonial alliances with material furnished by the most diverse philosophies and theologies, provided only they can find a place in their framework for its peculiar emotional mood. We have no right, therefore, to invoke its prestige as distinctively in favour of any special belief, such as that in absolute idealism, or in the absolute monistic identity, or in the absolute goodness, of the world. It is only relatively in favour of all these things — it passes out of common human consciousness in the direction in which they lie. ...

(3) Yet, I repeat once more, the existence of mystical states absolutely overthrows the pretension of non-mystical states to be the sole and ultimate dictators of what we may believe. As a rule, mystical states merely add a supersensuous meaning to the ordinary outward data of consciousness. They are excitements like the emotions of love or ambition, gifts to our spirit by means of which facts already objectively before us fall into a new expressiveness and make a new connection with our active life. They do not contradict these facts as such, or deny anything that our senses have immediately seized. It is the rationalistic critic rather who plays the part of denier in the controversy, and his denials have no strength, for there never can be a state of facts to which new meaning may not truthfully be added, provided the mind ascend to a more enveloping point of view. It must always remain an open question whether mystical states may not possibly be such superior points of view, windows through which the mind looks out upon a more extensive and inclusive world. The difference of the views seen from the different mystical windows need not prevent us from entertaining this supposition. The wider world would in that case prove to have a mixed constitution like that of this world, that is all. It would have its celestial and its infernal regions, its tempting and its saving moments, its valid experiences and its counterfeit ones, just as our world has them; but it would be a wider world all the same. We should have to use its experiences by selecting and subordinating and substituting just as is our custom in this ordinary naturalistic world; we should be liable to error just as we are now; yet the counting in of that wider world of meanings, and the serious dealing with it, might, in spite of all the perplexity, be indispensable stages in our approach to the final fullness of the truth.

OTHER CHARACTERISTICS

AMONG the buildings-out of religion which the mind spontaneously indulges in, the æsthetic motive must never be forgotten. I promised to say nothing of ecclesiastical systems in these lectures. I may be allowed, however, to put in a word at this point on the way in which their satisfaction of certain æsthetic needs contributes to their hold on human nature. Although some persons aim most at intellectual purity and simplification, for others *richness* is the supreme imaginative requirement. When one's mind is strongly of this type, an individual religion will hardly serve the purpose. The inner need is rather of something institutional and complex, majestic in the hierarchic inter-relatedness of its parts, with authority descending from stage to stage, and at every stage objects for adjectives of mystery and splendour, derived in the last resort from the Godhead who is the fountain and culmination of the system. One feels then as if in presence of some vast incrusted work of jewellery or architecture; one hears the multitudinous liturgical appeal; one gets the honorific vibration coming from every quarter. Compared with such a noble complexity, in which ascending and descending movements seem in no way to jar upon stability, in which no single item, however humble, is insignificant, because so many august institutions hold it in its place, how flat does evangelical Protestantism appear, how bare the atmosphere of those isolated religious lives whose boast it is that 'man in the bush with God may meet'. What a pulveriza-tion and levelling of what a gloriously piled-up structure! To an imagination used to the perspectives of dignity and glory, the naked gospel scheme seems to offer an almshouse for a palace.

It is much like the patriotic sentiment of those brought up in ancient empires. How many emotions must be frustrated of their object, when one gives up the titles of dignity, the crimson lights and blare of brass, the gold embroidery, the plumed troops, the fear and trembling, and puts up with a president in a black coat who shakes hands with you, and comes, it may be, from a 'home' upon a veldt or prairie with one sitting-room and a Bible on its centre-table. It pauperizes the monarchical imagination!

The strength of these æsthetic sentiments makes it rigorously impossible, it seems to me, that Protestantism, however superior in spiritual profundity it may be to Catholicism, should at the present day succeed in making many converts from the more venerable ecclesiasticism. The latter offers a so much richer pasturage and shade to the fancy, has so many cells with so many different kinds of honey, is so indulgent in its multiform appeals to human nature, that Protestantism will always show to Catholic eyes the almshouse physiognomy. The bitter negativity of it is to the Catholic mind incomprehensible. To intellectual Catholics many of the antiquated beliefs and practices to which the Church gives countenance are, if taken literally, as childish as they are to Protestants. But they are childish in the pleasing sense of 'childlike', – innocent and amiable, and worthy to be smiled on in consideration of the undeveloped condition of the dear people's intellects. To the Protestant, on the contrary, they are childish in the sense of being idiotic falsehoods. He must stamp out their delicate and lovable redundancy, leaving the Catholic to shudder at his literalness. He appears to the latter as morose as if he were some hard-eyed, numb, monotonous kind of reptile. The two will never understand each other – their centres of emotional energy are too different. Rigorous truth and human nature's intricacies are always in need of a mutual interpreter. So much for the æsthetic diversities of the religious consciousness.

CONCLUSIONS

SUMMING up in the broadest possible way the characteristics of the religious life, as we have found them, it includes the following beliefs:

(1) That the visible world is part of a more spiritual universe from which it draws its chief significance;

(2) That union or harmonious relation with that higher universe is our true end;

(3) That prayer or inner communion with the spirit thereof — be that spirit 'God' or 'law' — is a process wherein work is really done, and spiritual energy flows in and produces effects, psychological or material, within the phenomenal world. . . .

In illustrating these characteristics by documents, we have been literally bathed in sentiment. In re-reading my manuscript, I am almost appalled at the amount of emotionality which I find in it. After so much of this, we can afford to be dryer and less sympathetic in the rest of the work that lies before us. . . . We have now to exert [our] critical activity, and to [consider] how far, in the light of other sciences and in that of general philosophy, [the] beliefs [above defined] can be considered *true*.

There is a notion in the air about us that religion is probably only an anachronism, a case of 'survival', an atavistic relapse into a mode of thought which humanity in its more enlightened examples has outgrown; and this notion our religious anthropologists at present do little to counteract.

This view is so widespread at the present day that I must

consider it with some explicitness before I pass to my own conclusions. Let me call it the 'Survival theory', for brevity's sake.

The pivot round which the religious life, as we have traced it, revolves, is the interest of the individual in his private personal destiny. Religion, in short, is a monumental chapter in the history of human egotism. . . . Science, on the other hand, has ended by utterly repudiating the personal point of view. She catalogues her elements and records her laws indifferent as to what purpose may be shown forth by them, and constructs her theories quite careless of their bearing on human anxieties and fates. . . . It is impossible, in the present temper of the scientific imagination, to find in the driftings of the cosmic atoms, whether they work on the universal or on the particular scale, anything but a kind of aimless weather, doing and undoing, achieving no proper history, and leaving no result. Nature has no one distinguishable ultimate tendency with which it is possible to feel a sympathy. . . . The books of natural theology which satisfied the intellects of our grandfathers seem to us quite grotesque, representing, as they did, a God who conformed the largest things of nature to the paltriest of our private wants. The God whom science recognizes must be a God of universal laws exclusively, a God who does a wholesale, not a retail business. He cannot accommodate his processes to the convenience of individuals. . . .

You see how natural it is, from this point of view, to treat religion as a mere survival, for religion does in fact perpetuate the traditions of the most primeval thought. To coerce the spiritual powers, or to square them and get them on our side, was, during enormous tracts of time, the one great object in our dealings with the natural world. For our ancestors, dreams, hallucinations, revelations, and cock-and-bull stories were inextricably mixed with facts. Up to a comparatively recent date such distinctions as those between what has been verified and what is only conjectured, between the impersonal and the personal aspects of existence, were hardly suspected or conceived. Whatever you imagined in a lively manner, whatever you thought fit to be true, you affirmed confidently; and whatever you affirmed, your comrades believed. Truth was what had not yet been contradicted, most things were taken into the mind from the point of view of their human suggestiveness, and the attention confined itself exclusively to the æsthetic and dramatic aspects of events.

How indeed could it be otherwise? The extraordinary value, for explanation and prevision, of those mathematical and mechanical modes of conception which science uses, was a result that could not possibly have been expected in advance. Weight, movement, velocity, direction, position, what thin, pallid, uninteresting ideas! How could the richer animistic aspects of Nature, the peculiarities and oddities that make phenomena picturesquely striking or expressive, fail to have been first singled out and followed by philosophy as the more promising avenue to the knowledge of Nature's life? Well, it is still in these richer animistic and dramatic aspects that religion delights to dwell. It is the terror and beauty of phenomena, the 'promise' of the dawn and of the rainbow, the 'voice' of the thunder, the 'gentleness' of the summer rain, the 'sublimity' of the stars, and not the physical laws which these things follow, by which the religious mind still continues to be most impressed; and just as of yore, the devout man tells you that in the solitude of his room or of the fields he still feels the divine presence, that inflowings of help come in reply to his prayers, and that sacrifices to this unseen reality fill him with security and peace.

Pure anachronism! says the survival-theory; — anachronism for which deanthropomorphization of the imagination is the remedy required. The less we mix the private with the cosmic, the more we dwell in universal and impersonal terms, the truer heirs of Science we become.

In spite of the appeal which this impersonality of the scientific attitude makes to a certain magnanimity of temper, I believe it to be shallow, and I can now state my reason in comparatively few words. That reason is that, so long as we deal with the cosmic and the general, we deal only with the symbols of reality, but *as soon as we deal with private and personal phenomena as such, we deal with realities in the completest sense of the term.* I think I can easily make clear what I mean by these words.

The world of our experience consists at all times of two parts, an objective and a subjective part, of which the former may be incalculably more extensive than the latter, and yet the latter can never be omitted or suppressed. The objective part is the sum total of whatsoever at any given time we may be thinking of, the subjective part is the inner 'state' in which the thinking comes to pass. What we think of may be enormous, — the cosmic times and spaces, for example, — whereas the inner state may be the most fugitive and paltry activity of mind. Yet the cosmic objects, so far as the experience yields them, are but ideal pictures of something whose existence we do not inwardly possess but only point at outwardly, while the inner state is our very experience itself; its reality and that of our experience are one. . . .

It is absurd for science to say that the egotistic elements of experience should be suppressed. The axis of reality runs solely through the egotistic places, — they are strung upon it like so many beads. To describe the world with all the various feelings of the individual pinch of destiny, all the various spiritual attitudes, left out from the description — they being as describable as anything else — would be something like offering a printed bill of fare as the equivalent for a solid meal. Religion makes no such blunder. . . . The contention of the survival-theory that we ought to stick to non-personal elements exclusively seems like saying that we ought to be satisfied forever with reading the naked bill of fare. I think, therefore, that however particular questions connected with our individual destinies may be answered, it is only by acknowledging them as genuine questions, and living in the sphere of thought which they open up, that we become profound. But to live thus is to be religious; so I unhesitatingly repudiate the survival-theory of religion, as being founded on an egregious mistake. It does not follow, because our ancestors made so many errors of fact and mixed them with religion, that we should therefore leave off being religious at all. . . .

Let us agree, then, that Religion, occupying herself with personal destinies and keeping thus in contact with the only absolute realities which we know, must necessarily play an eternal part in human history. The next thing to decide is what she reveals about those destinies, or whether indeed she reveals anything distinct enough to be considered a general message to mankind. We have done, as you see, with our preliminaries, and our final summing up can now begin.

I am well aware that after all the palpitating documents which I have quoted, and all the perspectives of emotion-inspiring institution and belief that my previous lectures have opened, the dry analysis to which I now advance may appear to many of you like an anti-climax, a tapering-off and flattening out of the subject, instead of a crescendo of interest and result. I said awhile ago that the religious attitude of Protestants appears poverty-stricken to the Catholic imagination. Still more poverty-stricken, I fear, may my final summing up of the subject appear at first to some of you. On which account I pray you now to bear this point in mind, that in the present part of it I am expressly trying to reduce religion to its lowest admissible terms, to that minimum, free from individualistic excrescences, which all religions contain as their nucleus, and on which it may be hoped that all religious persons may agree. [The questions to be considered are:]

First, is there, under all the discrepancies of the creeds, a common nucleus to which they bear their testimony unanimously?

And second, ought we to consider the testimony true?

I will take up the first question first, and answer it immediately in the affirmative. The warring gods and formulæ of the various religions do indeed cancel each other, but there is a certain uniform deliverance in which religions all appear to meet. It consists of two parts:

(1) An uneasiness; and
(2) Its solution.

(1) The uneasiness, reduced to its simplest terms, is a sense that there is *something wrong about us* as we naturally stand.

(2) The solution is a sense that *we are saved from the wrongness* by making proper connection with the higher powers.

In those more developed minds which alone we are studying, the wrongness takes a moral character, and the salvation takes a mystical tinge. I think we shall keep well within the limits of what is common to all such minds if we formulate the essence of their religious experience in terms like these:

The individual, so far as he suffers from his wrongness and criticizes it, is to that extent consciously beyond it, and in at least possible touch with something higher, if anything higher exist. Along with the wrong part there is thus a better part of him, even though it may be but a most helpless germ. With which part he should identify his real being is by no means obvious at this stage; but when stage 2 (the stage of solution or salvation) arrives, the man identifies his real being with the germinal higher part of himself; and does so in the following way. *He becomes conscious that his higher part is conterminous and continuous with a* MORE *of the same quality, which is operative in the universe outside of him, and which he can keep in working touch with, and in a fashion get on board of and save himself when all his lower being has gone to pieces in the wreck.*

It seems to me that all the phenomena are accurately describable in these very simple general terms.... There is probably no autobiographic document, among all those which I have quoted, to which the description will not well apply. One need only add such specific details as will adapt it to various theologies and various personal temperaments, and one will then have the various experiences reconstructed in their individual forms.

So far, however, as this analysis goes, the experiences are only psychological phenomena, ... [though] they possess, it is true, enormous biological worth. ... I now turn to my second question: What is the objective 'truth' of their content?

The part of the content concerning which the question of truth most pertinently arises is that 'MORE of the same quality' with which our own higher self appears in the experience to come into harmonious working relation. Is such a 'more' merely our own notion, or does it really exist? If so, in what shape does it exist? Does it act, as well as exist? And in what form should we conceive of that 'union' with it of which religious geniuses are so convinced? . . .

What follows should be read in the light of the 'transmission hypothesis' (p. 72).

We shall do well to seek first of all a way of describing the 'more' which psychologists may also recognize as real. The *subconscious* [or subliminal] *self* is nowadays a well-accredited psychological entity; and I believe that in it we have exactly the mediating term required. Apart from all religious considerations, there is actually and literally more life in our total soul than we are at any time aware of. . . . Much of the content of this larger background against which our conscious being stands out in relief is insignificant. Imperfect memories, silly jingles, inhibitive timidities, 'dissolutive' phenomena of various sorts, as Myers calls them, enter into it for a large part. But in it many of the performances of genius seem also to have their origin; and in our study of conversion, of mystical experiences, and of prayer, we have seen how striking a part invasions from this region play in the religious life.

[This reference of the phenomena to a subconscious self must not be taken to exclude the possibility of the intervention of higher powers.] If there be higher spiritual agencies that can directly touch us, the psychological condition of their doing so might be our possession of a subconscious region which alone should yield access to them. The hubbub of the waking life might close a door which in the dreamy Subliminal might remain ajar or open. . . . Let me then propose, as an hypothesis, that whatever it may be on its *farther* side, the 'more' with which in religious experience we feel ourselves connected is on its *hither* side the subconscious continuation of our conscious life. . . .

This doorway into the subject seems to me the best one, for it mediates between a number of different points of view. Yet it is only a doorway, and difficulties present themselves as soon as we step through it, and ask how far our transmarginal consciousness carries us if we follow it on its remoter side. Here the over-beliefs begin. . . . Here the prophets of all the different religions come with their visions, voices, raptures, and other openings, supposed by each to authenticate his own peculiar faith. . . .

Disregarding the over-beliefs, and confining ourselves to what is common and generic, we have *in the fact that the conscious person is continuous with a wider self through which saving experiences come*, a positive content of religious experience which, it seems to me, *is literally and objectively true as far as it goes*. If I now proceed to state my own hypothesis about the farther limits of this extension of our personality, I shall be offering my own over-belief — though I know it will appear a sorry under-belief to some of you — for which I can only bespeak the same indulgence which in a converse case I should accord to yours.

The further limits of our being plunge, it seems to me, into an altogether other dimension of existence from the sensible and merely 'understandable' world. . . . The whole drift of my education goes to persuade me that the world of our present consciousness is only one out of many worlds of consciousness that exist, and that those other worlds must contain experiences which have a meaning for our life also; and that although in the main their experiences and those of this world keep discrete, yet the two become continuous at certain points, and higher energies filter in. . . . I *can*, of course, put myself into the sectarian scientist's attitude, and imagine vividly that the world of sensations and of scientific laws and objects may be all. But whenever I do this, I hear that inward monitor of which W. K. Clifford once wrote, whispering the word 'bosh!' Humbug is humbug, even though it bear the scientific name, and the total expression of human experience, as I view it objectively, invincibly urges me beyond the narrow 'scientific' bounds.

> In a broad sense, the wider reality with which we feel ourselves in contact may be identified with the 'God' of popular theology: but in a concluding chapter, James makes it clear that his view differs in many respects from what he has elsewhere called 'anthropomorphic monarchical Theism'. 'The "omnipotent" and "omniscient" God of theology,' as he said in a letter, 'I regard as a disease of the philosophy shop'.

The ideal power with which we feel ourselves in connection, the 'God' of ordinary men, is, both by ordinary men and by philosophers, endowed with certain ... metaphysical attributes. . . . He is assumed as a matter of course to be 'one and only' and to be 'infinite'; and the notion of many finite gods is one which hardly anyone thinks it worth while to consider, and still less to uphold. Nevertheless, in the interests of intellectual clearness, I feel bound to say that religious experience, as we have studied it, cannot be cited as unequivocally supporting the monistic and infinitist belief. The only thing that it unequivocally testifies to is that we can experience union with *something* larger than ourselves and in that union find our greatest peace. Philosophy, with its passion for unity, and mysticism with its monoideistic bent, both 'pass to the limit' and identify the something with a unique God who is the all-inclusive soul of the world. Popular opinion, respectful to their authority, follows the example which they set.

Meanwhile the practical needs and experiences of religion seem to me sufficiently met by the belief that beyond each man and in a fashion continuous with him there exists a larger power which is friendly to him and to his ideals. All that the facts require is that the power should be both other and larger than our conscious selves. Anything larger will do, if only it be large enough to trust for the next step. It need not be infinite, it need not be solitary. It might conceivably even be only a larger and more godlike self, of which the present self would then be but the mutilated expression, and the universe might conceivably be a collection of such selves, of different degrees of inclusiveness, with no absolute unity realized in it at all. . . .

[This frankly pluralist outlook avoids the difficulty which is fundamental to all monistic hypotheses, whether they postulate a perfect and all-inclusive Absolute or a unique, omnipotent God.] On the monistic . . . view, evil, like everything else, must have its foundation in God; and the difficulty is to see how this can possibly be the case if God be absolutely good.[5] This difficulty faces us in every form of philosophy in which the world appears as one flawless unit of fact. . . . The philosophy of absolute

---

5. [Editor's footnote.] James discusses this fundamental difficulty more fully in an essay 'The Dilemma of Determinism' (which would have been more accurately entitled 'The Dilemma of Monism'). To quote from this essay: 'Your own studies have sufficiently shown you the almost desperate difficulty of making the notion that there is a single principle of things, and that principle absolute perfection, rhyme together with our daily vision of the facts of life. If perfection be the principle, how comes there any imperfection here? If God be good, how came he to create . . . the devil? The evil facts must be explained as seeming, the devil must be whitewashed . . . if neither God's goodness nor his unity and power are to remain impugned.' But 'when, for example, I imagine such carrion as the Brockton murder, I cannot conceive

idealism, so vigorously represented both in Scotland and America to-day, has to struggle with [it] quite as much as scholastic theism struggled in its time; and although it would be premature to say that there is no speculative issue whatever from the puzzle, it is perfectly fair to say that there is no clear or easy issue, and that the only *obvious* escape from paradox here is to cut loose from the monistic assumption altogether, and to allow the world to have existed from its origin in pluralistic form, as an aggregate or collection of higher and lower things and principles, rather than an absolutely unitary fact. For then evil would not need to be essential; it might be, and may always have been, an independent portion that had no rational or absolute right to live with the rest, and which we might conceivably hope to see got rid of at last. . . .

Here we have the . . . notion fairly and squarely presented to us, of there being elements of the universe which may make no rational whole in conjunction with the other elements, and which, from the point of view of any system which those other elements make up, can only be considered so much irrelevance and accident – so much 'dirt', as it were, and matter out of place. I ask you now not to forget this notion; for although most philosophers seem either to forget it or to disdain it too much ever to mention

it as an act by which the universe, as a whole, logically and necessarily expresses its nature without shrinking from complicity with such a whole. And I deliberately refuse to keep on terms of loyalty with the universe by saying blankly that the murder, since it does flow from the nature of the whole, is not carrion. There are *some* instinctive reactions which I, for one, will not tamper with.' (*The Will to Believe*, pp. 166–7, 177–8.)

The orthodox explanation of 'such carrion as the Brockton murder' is, of course, to attribute it to man's misuse of the divine gift of freewill. But the evil in the universe cannot all be explained away in this fashion. Human volitions have nothing to do with such facts as that animals prey on one another for food, that cats are directed by their instinctive constitution to torture mice before killing them, etc. (Cf. p. 200.)

it, I believe that we shall have to admit it . . . as containing an element of truth. . . .

I think, in fact, that a final philosophy of religion will have to consider the pluralistic hypothesis more seriously than it has hitherto been willing to consider it.

MISCELLANEOUS
WRITINGS

Miscellaneous Writings

INTEREST AND EFFORT IN EDUCATION

FROM *Talks to Teachers*

AMONG the recent modern reforms of teaching methods, a certain disparagement of emulation, as a laudable spring of action in the schoolroom, has often made itself heard. More than a century ago, Rousseau, in his *Emile*, branded rivalry between one pupil and another as too base a passion to play a part in an ideal education. . . . But to veto and taboo all possible rivalry of one youth with another, because such rivalry may degenerate into greedy and selfish excess, does seem to savour somewhat of sentimentality, or even of fanaticism. The feeling of rivalry lies at the very basis of our being, all social improvement being largely due to it. There is a noble and generous kind of rivalry, as well as a spiteful and greedy kind; and the noble and generous form is particularly common in childhood. All games owe the zest which they bring with them to the fact that they are rooted in the emulous passion, yet they are the chief means of training in fairness and magnanimity. Can the teacher afford to throw such an ally away? Ought we seriously to hope that marks, distinctions, prizes, and other goals of effort, based on the pursuit of recognized superiority, should be forever banished from our schools? As a psychologist, obliged to notice the deep and pervasive character of the emulous passion, I must confess my doubts.

The wise teacher will use this instinct as he uses others, reaping its advantages, and appealing to it in such a way as to reap a maximum of benefit with a minimum of harm;

for, after all, we must confess, with a French critic of Rousseau's doctrine, that the deepest spring of action in us is the sight of action in another. The spectacle of effort is what awakens and sustains our own effort. No runner running all alone on a race-track will find in his own will the power of stimulation which his rivalry with other runners incites, when he feels them at his heels, about to pass. When a trotting horse is 'speeded', a running horse must go beside him to keep him to the pace.

As imitation slides into emulation, so emulation slides into *Ambition;* and ambition connects itself closely with *Pugnacity* and *Pride....* Pride and pugnacity have often been considered unworthy passions to appeal to in the young. But in their more refined and noble forms they play a great part in the schoolroom and in education generally, being in some characters most potent spurs to effort. Pugnacity need not be thought of merely in the form of physcial combativeness. It can be taken in the sense of a general unwillingness to be beaten by any kind of difficulty. It is what makes us feel 'stumped' and challenged by arduous achievements, and is essential to a spirited and enterprising character. We have of late been hearing much of the philosophy of tenderness in education; 'interest' must be assiduously awakened in everything, difficulties must be smoothed away. *Soft* pedagogics have taken the place of the old steep and rocky path to learning. But from this lukewarm air the bracing oxygen of effort is left out. It is nonsense to suppose that every step in education *can* be interesting. The fighting impulse must often be appealed to. Make the pupil feel ashamed of being scared at fractions, of being 'downed' by the law of falling bodies; rouse his pugnacity and pride, and he will rush at the difficult places with a sort of inner wrath at himself that is one of his best moral faculties. A victory scored under such conditions becomes a turning-point and crisis of his character. It represents the high-water mark of his powers, and serves thereafter as an ideal pattern for his self-imitation. The teacher who never rouses this sort of pugnacious excitement in his pupils falls short of one of his best forms of usefulness.

No topic has received more attention from pedagogical writers than that of interest. . . . Since some objects are natively interesting and in others interest is artificially acquired, the teacher must know which the natively interesting ones are; for, as we shall see immediately, other objects can artificially acquire an interest only through first becoming associated with some of these natively interesting things.

The native interests of children lie altogether in the sphere of sensation. Novel things to look at or novel sounds to hear, especially when they involve the spectacle of action of a violent sort, will always divert the attention from abstract conceptions of objects verbally taken in. The grimace that Johnny is making, the spitballs that Tommy is ready to throw, the dog-fight in the street, or the distant firebells ringing, – these are the rivals with which the teacher's powers of being interesting have incessantly to cope. . . .

Living things, then, moving things, or things that savour of danger or of blood, that have a dramatic quality, – these are the objects natively interesting to childhood, to the exclusion of almost everything else; and the teacher of young children, until more artificial interests have grown up, will keep in touch with her pupils by constant appeal to such matters as these. Instruction must be carried on objectively, experimentally, anecdotally. The blackboard-drawing and story-telling must constantly come in. But, of course, these methods cover only the first steps, and carry one but a little way.

Can we now formulate any general principle by which the later and more artificial interests connect themselves with these early ones that the child brings with him to the school?

Fortunately, we can: there is a very simple law that relates the acquired and the native interests with each other.

Any object not interesting in itself may become interesting through becoming associated with an object in which an interest already exists. The two associated objects grow, as it were, together: the interesting portion sheds its quality over the whole; and thus things not interesting in their own right borrow an interest which becomes as real and as strong as that of any natively interesting thing. . . .

This is one of the most striking proofs of the range of application of the principle of association of ideas in psychology. An idea will infect another with its own emotional interest when they have become both associated together into any sort of a mental total. . . .

You will understand this abstract statement easily if I take the most frequent of concrete examples, – the interest which things borrow from their connection with our own personal welfare. . . . The moment a thing becomes connected with the fortunes of the self, it forthwith becomes an interesting thing. Lend the child his books, pencils, and other apparatus: then give them to him, make them his own, and notice the new light with which they instantly shine in his eyes. He takes a new kind of care of them altogether. In mature life, all the drudgery of a man's business or profession, intolerable in itself, is shot through with engrossing significance because he knows it to be associated with his personal fortunes. . . . *From all these facts there emerges a very simple abstract programme for the teacher to follow in keeping the attention of the child : Begin with the line of his native interests, and offer him objects that have some immediate connection with these.* The kindergarten methods, the object-teaching routine, the blackboard and manual-training work, – all recognize this feature. Schools in which these methods preponderate are schools where discipline is easy, and where the voice of the master claiming order and attention in threatening tones need never be heard.

Next, step by step, connect with these first objects and experiences the later objects and ideas which you wish to instil. Associate the new with the old in some natural and telling way, so that the interest, being shed along from point to point, finally suffuses the entire system of objects of thought. This is the abstract statement; and, abstractly, nothing can be easier to understand. It is in the fulfilment of the rule that the difficulty lies; for the difference between an interesting and a tedious teacher consists in little more than the inventiveness by which the one is able to mediate these associations and connections, and in the dullness in discovering such transitions which the other shows. One teacher's mind will fairly coruscate with points of connection between the new lesson and the circumstances of the children's other experience. Anecdotes and reminiscences will abound in her talk; and the shuttle of interest will shoot backward and forward, weaving the new and the old together in a lively and entertaining way. Another teacher has no such inventive fertility, and his lesson will always be a dead and heavy thing. This is the psychological meaning of the Herbartian principle of 'preparation' for each lesson, and of correlating the new with the old. It is the psychological meaning of that whole method of concentration in studies of which you have recently been hearing so much. When the geography and English and history and arithmetic simultaneously make cross-references to one another, you get an interesting set of processes all along the line.

A certain doubt may now occur to some of you. A while ago, apropos of the pugnacious instinct, I spoke of our modern pedagogy as being possibly too 'soft'. You may perhaps here face me with my own words, and ask whether the exclusive effort on the teacher's part to keep the pupil's spontaneous interest going, and to avoid the more strenuous path of voluntary attention to repulsive work, does not savour also of sentimentalism. The greater part of school-room work, you say, must, in the nature of things, always be repulsive. To face uninteresting drudgery is a good part of life's work. Why seek to eliminate it from the school-room or minimize the sterner law?

A word or two will obviate what might perhaps become a serious misunderstanding here.

It is certain that most schoolroom work, till it has become habitual and automatic, is repulsive, and cannot be done without voluntarily jerking back the attention to it every now and then. This is inevitable, let the teacher do what he will. It flows from the inherent nature of the subjects and of the learning mind. The repulsive processes of verbal memorizing, of discovering steps of mathematical identity, and the like, must borrow their interest at first from purely external sources, mainly from the personal interests with which success in mastering them is associated, such as gaining of rank, avoiding punishment, not being beaten by a difficulty and the like. Without such borrowed interest, the child could not attend to them at all.

But in these processes what becomes interesting enough to be attended to is not thereby attended to *without effort*. Effort always has to go on, derived interest, for the most part, not awakening attention that is *easy*, however spontaneous it may now have to be called. The interest which the teacher, by his utmost skill, can lend to the subject, proves over and over again to be only an interest sufficient *to let loose the effort*. The teacher, therefore, need never concern himself about *inventing* occasions where effort must be called into play. Let him still awaken whatever sources of interest in the subject he can by stirring up connections between it and the pupil's nature, whether in the line of theoretic curiosity, of personal interest, or of pugnacious impulse. The laws of mind will then bring enough pulses of effort into play to keep the pupil exercised in the direction of the subject. There is, in fact, no greater school of effort than the steady struggle to attend to immediately repulsive or difficult objects of thought which have grown to interest us through their association as means, with some remote ideal end.

The Herbartian doctrine of interest ought not, therefore, in principle to be reproached with making pedagogy soft. If it do so, it is because it is unintelligently carried on. Do not, then, for the mere sake of discipline, command attention from your pupils in thundering tones. Do not too often beg it from them as a favour, nor claim it as a right, nor try habitually to excite it by preaching the importance of the subject. Sometimes, indeed, you must do these things; but, the more you have to do them, the less skilful teacher you will show yourself to be. Elicit interest from within, by the warmth with which you care for the topic yourself, and by following the laws I have laid down.

REMARKS AT THE PEACE BANQUET

AND

THE MORAL EQUIVALENT OF WAR

THE *Remarks at the Peace Banquet* were delivered at
the Universal Peace Congress held in Boston in 1904.
Their theme was more fully developed in *The Moral
Equivalent of War*, which was written for, and first
published by, the Association for International Conciliation in 1910. Both are now published in *Memories and Studies* (1911). The two opening paragraphs
of the extracts that follow are taken from the first
source, and the remainder from the second.

I am only a philosopher, and there is only one thing that a
philosopher can be relied on to do, and that is to contradict
other philosophers. In ancient times philosophers defined
man as the rational animal; and philosophers since then
have always found much more to say about the rational
than about the animal part of the definition. But looked at
candidly, reason bears about the same proportion to the rest
of human nature that we in this hall bear to the rest of
America, Europe, Asia, Africa and Polynesia. Reason is
one of the very feeblest of nature's forces, if you take it only
at one spot and moment. It is only in the very long run that
its effects become perceptible. Reason assumes to settle
things by weighing them against each other without prejudice, partiality or excitement; but what affairs in the
concrete are settled by is, and always will be, just prejudices,
partialities, cupidities and excitements. Appealing to reason
as we do, we are in a sort of forlorn-hope situation, like a

small sandbank in the midst of a hungry sea ready to wash it out of existence. But sandbanks grow when the conditions favour; and weak as reason is, it has this unique advantage over its antagonists that its activity never lets up and that it presses always in one direction, while men's prejudices vary, their passions ebb and flow, and their excitements are intermittent. Our sandbank, I absolutely believe, is bound to grow. Bit by bit it will get dyked and breakwatered. But sitting as we do in this warm room, with music and lights and smiling faces, it is easy to get too sanguine about our task; and since I am called to speak I feel as if it might not be out of place to say a word about the strength of our enemy.

Our permanent enemy is the rooted bellicosity of human nature. Man, biologically considered, and whatever else he may be into the bargain, is the most formidable of all beasts of prey, and, indeed, the only one that preys systematically on his own species. We are once for all adapted to the military status. A millennium of peace would not breed the fighting disposition out of our bone and marrow, and a function so ingrained and vital will never consent to die without resistance, and will always find impassioned apologists and idealizers. . . .

At the present day, civilized opinion is a curious mental mixture. The military instincts and ideals are as strong as ever, but are confronted by reflective criticisms which sorely curb their ancient freedom. . . . It is plain that on this subject civilized man has developed a sort of double personality. If we take European nations, no legitimate interest of any one of them would seem to justify the tremendous destructions which a war to compass it would necessarily entail. It would seem as though common-sense and reason ought to find a way to reach agreement in every conflict of honest interests. I myself think it our bounden duty to believe in such international rationality as possible. But, as things stand, I see how desperately hard it is to bring the peace-party and the war-party together, and I believe that the difficulty is due to certain deficiencies in the programme of pacificism which set the militarist imagination strongly, and to a certain extent justifiably, against it. In the whole discussion both sides are on imaginative and sentimental ground. It is but one utopia against another, and everything one says must be abstract and hypothetical. Subject to this criticism and caution, I will try to characterize in abstract strokes the opposite imaginative forces, and point out what to my own very fallible mind seems the best utopian hypothesis, the most promising line of conciliation. . . .

Reflective apologists for war at the present day all take it religiously. It is a sort of sacrament. Its profits are to the vanquished as well as to the victor; and quite apart from any question of profit, it is an absolute good, we are told, for it is human nature at its highest dynamic. Its 'horrors' are a cheap price to pay for rescue from the only alternative supposed, of a world of clerks and teachers, of co-education and zoophily, of 'consumer's leagues' and 'associated charities', of industrialism unlimited, and feminism unabashed. No scorn, no hardness, no valour any more! Fie upon such a cattleyard of a planet!

So far as the central essence of this feeling goes, no healthy-minded person, it seems to me, can help to some degree partaking of it. Militarism is the great preserver of our ideals of hardihood, and human life with no use for hardihood would be contemptible. Without risks or prizes for the darer, history would be insipid indeed; and there is a type of military character which everyone feels the race should never cease to breed, for everyone is sensitive to its superiority. The duty is incumbent on mankind, of keeping military characters in stock — of keeping them, if not for use, then as ends in themselves and as pure pieces of perfection, — so that Roosevelt's weaklings and mollycoddles may not end by making everything else disappear from the face of nature.

This natural sort of feeling forms, I think, the innermost soul of army-writings . . . The *Philosophie des Krieges* by S. R. Steinmetz is a good example. War, according to this author, is an ordeal instituted by God, who weighs the nations in its balance. . . . [The] upshot [of the book] can, it seems to me, be summed up in Simon Patten's word, that mankind was nursed in pain and fear, and that the transition to a 'pleasure-economy' may be fatal to a being wielding no powers of defence against its disintegrative influences. If we speak of the *fear of emancipation from the fear-régime*, we put the whole situation into a single phrase; fear regarding ourselves now taking the place of the ancient fear of the enemy.

Turn the fear over as I will in my mind, it all seems to lead back to two unwillingnesses of the imagination, one æsthetic, the other moral; unwillingness, first to envisage a future in which army-life, with its many elements of charm, shall be for ever impossible, and in which the destinies of peoples shall never more be decided quickly, thrillingly, and tragically, by force, but only gradually and insipidly by 'evolution'; and, secondly, unwillingness to see the supreme theatre of human strenuousness closed, and the splendid military aptitudes of men doomed to keep always in a state of latency and never show themselves in action. These insistent unwillingnesses, no less than other æsthetic and ethical insistencies, have, it seems to me, to be listened to and respected. One cannot meet them effectively by mere counter-insistence on war's expensiveness and horror. The horror makes the thrill; and when the question is of getting the extremest and supremest out of human nature, talk of expense sounds ignominious. The weakness of so much merely negative criticism is evident – pacificism makes no converts from the military party. The military party denies neither the bestiality nor the horror, nor the expense; it only says that these things tell but half the story. It only says that war is *worth* them; that, taking human nature as a whole, its wars are its best protection against its weaker and more cowardly self, and that man cannot *afford* to adopt a peace-economy.

Pacificists ought to enter more deeply into the æsthetical and ethical point of view of their opponents. . . . So long as anti-militarists propose no substitute for war's disciplinary function, no *moral equivalent* of war, analogous, as one might say, to the mechanical equivalent of heat, so long they fail to realize the full inwardness of the situation. And as a rule they do fail. The duties, penalties, and sanctions pictured in the utopias they paint are all too weak and tame to touch the military-minded. . . . This weakness pervades all the socialistic literature with which I am acquainted. Even in Lowes Dickinson's exquisite dialogue,[1] high wages and short hours are the only forces invoked for overcoming man's distaste for repulsive kinds of labour. Meanwhile men at large still live as they always have lived, under a pain-and-fear economy – for those of us who live in an ease-economy are but an island in the stormy ocean – and the whole atmosphere of present-day utopian literature tastes mawkish and dishwatery to people who still keep a sense for life's more bitter flavours. It suggests, in truth, ubiquitous inferiority.

Inferiority is always with us, and merciless scorn of it is the keynote of the military temper. 'Dogs, would you live for ever?' shouted Frederick the Great. 'Yes', say our

1. *Justice and Liberty*, New York, 1909.

utopians, 'let us live forever, and raise our level gradually.' The best thing about our 'inferiors' to-day is that they are as tough as nails, and physically and morally almost as insensitive. Utopianism would see them soft and squeamish, while militarism would keep their callousness, but transfigure it into a meritorious characteristic, needed by 'the service', and redeemed by that from the suspicion of inferiority. All the qualities of a man acquire dignity when he knows that the service of the collectivity that owns him needs them. If proud of the collectivity, his own pride rises in proportion. No collectivity is like an army for nourishing such pride; but it has to be confessed that the only sentiment which the image of pacific cosmopolitan industrialism is capable of arousing in countless worthy breasts is shame at the idea of belonging to *such* a collectivity. It is obvious that the United States of America as they exist to-day impress a mind like General Lee's as so much human blubber. Where is the sharpness and precipitousness, the contempt for life, whether one's own or another's? Where is the savage 'yes' and 'no', the unconditional duty? Where is the conscription? Where is the blood-tax? Where is anything that one feels honoured by belonging to?

Having said thus much in preparation, I will now confess my own utopia. I devoutly believe in the reign of peace and in the gradual advent of some sort of a socialistic equilibrium. The fatalistic view of the war-function is to me nonsense, for I know that war-making is due to definite motives, and subject to prudential checks and reasonable criticisms, just like any other form of enterprise. And when whole nations are the armies, and the science of destruction vies in intellectual refinement with the sciences of production, I see that war becomes absurd and impossible from its own monstrosity. . . .

All these beliefs of mine put me squarely into the anti-militarist party. But I do not believe that peace either ought to be or will be permanent on this globe, unless the states pacifically organized preserve some of the old elements of army-discipline. A permanently successful peace-economy cannot be a simple pleasure-economy. In the more or less socialistic future towards which mankind seems to be drifting, we must still subject ourselves collectively to those severities which answer to our real position upon this only partly hospitable globe. We must make new energies and hardihoods continue the manliness to which the military mind so faithfully clings. Martial virtues must be the enduring cement; intrepidity, contempt of softness, surrender of private interest, obedience to command, must still remain the rock upon which states are built – unless, indeed, we wish for dangerous reactions against commonwealths fit only for contempt, and liable to invite attack whenever a centre of crystallization for military-minded enterprise gets formed anywhere in their neighbourhood.

The war-party is assuredly right in affirming and re-affirming that the martial virtues, although originally gained by the race through war, are absolute and permanent human goods. Patriotic pride and ambition in their military form are, after all, only specifications of a more general competitive passion. They are its first form, but that is no reason for supposing them to be its last form. Men now are proud of belonging to a conquering nation, and without a murmur they lay down their persons and their wealth, if, by so doing, they may fend off subjection.... Why should men not some day feel that it is worth a blood-tax to belong to a collectivity superior in *any* ideal respect? Why should they not blush with indignant shame if the community that owns them is vile in any way whatsoever? Individuals, daily more numerous, now feel this civic passion. It is only a question of blowing on the spark till the whole population gets incandescent, and on the ruins of the old morals of military honour, a stable system of morals of civic honour builds itself up.

Let me illustrate my idea more concretely. There is nothing to make one indignant in the mere fact that life is hard, that men should toil and suffer pain. The planetary conditions once for all are such, and we can stand it. But that so many men, by mere accidents of birth and opportunity, should have a life of *nothing else* but toil and pain and hardness and inferiority imposed upon them, should have *no* vacation, while others natively no more deserving never get any taste of this campaigning life at all, – *this* is capable of arousing indignation in reflective minds. It may end by seeming shameful to all of us that some of us have nothing but campaigning, and others nothing but unmanly ease. If now – and this is my idea – there were, instead of military conscription, a conscription of the whole youthful population to form for a certain number of years a part of the army enlisted against *Nature*, the injustice would tend to be evened out, and numerous other goods to the commonwealth would follow. The military ideas of hardihood and discipline would be wrought into the growing fibre of the people; no-one would remain blind, as the luxurious classes now are blind, to man's relations to the globe he lives on, and to the permanently sour and hard foundations of his higher life. To coal and iron mines, to freight trains, to fishing fleets in December, to dish-washing, clothes-washing, and window-washing, to road-building and tunnel-making, to foundries and stokeholes, and to the frames of skyscrapers, would our gilded youth be drafted off, according to their choice, to get the childishness knocked out of them, and to come back into society with healthier sympathies and soberer ideas. They would have

paid their blood-tax, done their own part in the immemorial human warfare against nature; they would tread the
earth more proudly, the women would value them more
highly, they would be better fathers and teachers of the
following generation.

Such a conscription, with the state of public opinion that
would have required it, and the many moral fruits it would
bear, would preserve in the midst of a pacific civilization
the manly virtues which the military party is so afraid of
seeing disappear in peace. We should get toughness without
callousness, authority with as little criminal cruelty as
possible, and painful work done cheerily because the duty
is temporary, and threatens not, as now, to degrade the
whole remainder of one's life. I spoke of the 'moral equivalent' of war. So far, war has been the only force that can
discipline a whole community, and until an equivalent
discipline is organized, I believe that war must have its
way. But I have no serious doubt that the ordinary prides
and shames of social man, once developed to a certain intensity, are capable of organizing such a moral equivalent as I
have sketched. . . . It is but a question of time, of skilful
propagandism, and of opinion-making men seizing historic
opportunities.

New Pelicans
and other books are
described on the
last few pages

THE QUEEN'S GOVERNMENT
Sir Ivor Jennings, Q.C.

A292

SIR IVOR JENNINGS, who has recently been elected Master of Trinity Hall, Cambridge, is perhaps the best-known and most authoritative writer on British constitutional law and practice. His new work, specially written for Pelican Books, lucidly and brilliantly describes, in non-technical language, the principles of British democracy and its institutions.

The unique British combination of liberty and law, and its maintenance and expression in the Monarchy, Parliament, the working of Cabinet Government and the Executive, the political system behind them, and the bases and operation of law enforcement and the administration of justice, are all covered and summarized in this survey of the machinery of national and public life. (2s 6d)

THE PELICAN PHILOSOPHY SERIES

ETHICS

P. H. Nowell-Smith

A293

'WHAT ought I to do, here and now?' This is a question which each of us frequently has to answer. More rarely, in a reflective moment or when faced with a difficult moral problem, we ask such questions as: 'What ought I to do in general?', 'To what moral code ought I to adhere?', 'Why should I adhere to any moral code at all?' These are the perennial questions of moral philosophy.

The aim of this book is not to answer these questions, to provide a handbook in which solutions to the practical problems of life can be looked up. It has been written on the assumption that our practical thinking is often less efficient than it might be because we do not fully understand the words and concepts that we use. Its purpose is to make clear the complicated connexions between such words as 'good', 'right', 'ought', 'choose', 'duty', 'desire' and 'pleasure'. The author has applied to moral language some of the recent discoveries made in logic; but the concepts discussed are the traditional concepts of ethics. (3s 6d)

A list of the other books available in

THE PELICAN PHILOSOPHY SERIES

is on the inside back cover of this book

DREAMS AND NIGHTMARES
J. A. Hadfield
A294

DREAMS have a fascination for everyone, partly because of their bizarre nature, partly because these strange imaginings come from within ourselves, and partly because of the effect they have upon our daily lives. It is not surprising that efforts at dream interpretation have been made throughout all ages, by the most primitive tribes, who regard them as premonitions, no less than in the attempts at establishing a scientific method made by Freud with his sexual wish-fulfilment theory, Jung with his archetypes from the racial unconscious, and Adler with his urge to power. In this book, Dr Hadfield attempts to show that dreams have a biological role, and may be useful in the solution of the practical everyday, as well as of the deep-rooted, problems of our life. Many mathematical problems have been solved in dreams, and many scientific discoveries made by their means. We cannot, therefore, afford to ignore the significance of our dreaming, just as we cannot afford to ignore that of our intuition. This book, then, is a brief sketch of the mechanism, nature, and importance of our dream life.   (2s)

A list of the other books available in
THE PELICAN PSYCHOLOGY SERIES
is on the inside back cover of this book

THE LITERATURE OF THE UNITED STATES

Marcus Cunliffe

A289

The Literature of the United States in not intended as a textbook or work of reference, but as a general introduction to the main themes and figures of the American literary scene, from colonial times to the present day. Literature is to some extent treated as an expression of American character and experience. Thus, the problems faced by American writers *as Americans* are stressed throughout. However, it is suggested – especially in the concluding chapters – that the division between American and European literary qualities has been unfortunate, though understandable; and that it is a sign of American cultural maturity that the division is now less insisted upon than formerly. A table of dates in American history is appended, and the *Notes on Further Reading* are designed to lead those interested to a fuller acquaintance with the subject. (3s 6d)

Among American writers whose work has been published in Penguins are Edgar Alan Poe, Mark Twain, Henry James, Ernest Hemingway, F. Scott Fitzgerald, John Steinbeck, Sinclair Lewis, Elmer Rice, James Thurber, and many others.

THE PENGUIN BOOK
OF MODERN AMERICAN VERSE

Edited by Geoffrey Moore

D22

THIS is the first anthology of its kind to originate in Great Britain. It is designed to introduce the non-American reader to the range and variety of American poetry, and it presents as comprehensive a survey as possible of the twentieth-century poetic scene in the United States.

Both poets and their works are arranged in chronological order. The editor's starting-point has been the poet rather than the poem, and wherever possible selections have been chosen to illustrate the various phases of a poet's development. In addition to a general introduction there are notes on each contributor. Since many of the names included here will be unfamiliar outside the United States, these notes are quite full and contain critical comment as well as biographical and bibliographical information.

In this collection will be found not only such established figures as Ezra Pound, Robert Frost, and Wallace Stevens, but also the best of the most recent poets, some of whom have not previously appeared before in anthologies, even in the United States. It does not however include ballads and folk songs, for these belong to a different *genre*. (3s 6d)

PSYCHIATRY TO-DAY
David Stafford-Clark

A262

FOR better or worse, psychiatry is news to-day: it is also frequently a feature of entertainment on the films, on television, on the radio, and provides a theme for books and a plot for plays. Although it is one of the fundamental branches of medicine it has always achieved notoriety more readily than fame, and seems all too often to promise more than it can perform. What was once a forbidden mystery is in danger of becoming a popular fad.

This is a book about psychiatry written by a doctor for interested laymen: written, in the author's own words, to tell 'something of the practical possibilities of psychiatry, something of the size of the problem with which it has to deal, something of the spirit in which the psychiatrist approaches it, and something of the solid and sensible help which it is his aim and duty to provide....'

It deals vividly and lucidly with the historical background, the realities of normal and abnormal mental life, the present state of knowledge about causes, and the various techniques of treatment, as well as the theories on which they are based. It covers the results of treatment, the needs of the future and some plans for meeting them, and the wider implications of psychiatry in medicine as a whole, and in society.   (2s 6d)